TOO GREAT EXPECTATIONS

Too Great Expectations

THE ACADEMIC OUTLOOK OF YOUNG CHILDREN

DORIS R. ENTWISLE AND
LESLIE ALEC HAYDUK

THE JOHNS HOPKINS UNIVERSITY PRESS
Baltimore and London

Copyright © 1978 by The Johns Hopkins University Press

All rights reserved. No part of this book may be
reproduced or transmitted in any form or by any means,
electronic or mechanical, including photocopying,
recording, xerography, or any information storage and
retrieval system, without permission in writing
from the publisher.

Manufactured in the United States of America

The Johns Hopkins University Press, Baltimore, Maryland 21218
The Johns Hopkins Press Ltd., London

Library of Congress Catalog Card Number 77-23344
ISBN 0-8018-1986-5 ✓

Library of Congress Cataloging in Publication data
will be found on the last printed page of this book.

To our parents,

Charles and Helen Roberts

Alec and Alice Hayduk

Contents

Tables

Figures

Preface

This monograph is the outgrowth of seven years' work. Starting in 1969, several exploratory studies were undertaken prior to gathering data in the years 1971 to 1973 and framing the subsequent analysis. Some of the initial investigations were fruitless but others produced techniques for measuring children's expectations and gathering the other data reported here. Field experiments carried out from 1969 through 1974 led us toward many additional insights. The experiments themselves are reported elsewhere (see Entwisle and Webster, 1974a, 1974b), but there is a close tie between them and this observational study. They involved measuring the results of raising children's expectations and represented the first experimental work known to us where *young* children's academic expectations were the target variable. This book presents naturalistic observations that complement the experimental studies.

Our study describes children belonging to the first three cohorts of a larger longitudinal study. Each "cohort" is the entire first-grade class entering a given school in a particular year—usually three or four classrooms of children. Two of the cohorts described in this book were followed as they progressed through first grade. The third cohort was followed through both the first and second grades. We plan to continue studying these children until they complete third grade.

We are also using the strategies reported in this book to study other cohorts of children over comparable three-year time spans. Eventually we hope to describe what happens to children as they go through the first three grades in three different locales: a middle-class white neighborhood, an integrated (60 percent black) neighborhood of lower socioeconomic status, and an all-black neighborhood of lower socioeconomic status. (Of the results thus far obtained, only those for the white and integrated neighborhoods are given in this book.)

The reader will see that this book raises as many questions as it answers. We intend to pursue these questions as the more complete and extensive data become available.

We mark it a priviledge to have been associated with Murray Webster in the early stages of this work. He has done a great deal to help us, especially through his own experiments and theoretical insights. Other colleagues have contributed valuable suggestions and ideas: Muriel Berkeley, Sylvia Brown, Marguerite Bryan, Stauros Daoutis, Ellen Dickstein,

Susan Doering, Robert Gordon, Esther Grief, Robert Hogan, Judy Kennedy, Mary Klingmeyer, Eileen Rudert, and Michael Swafford.

A very special debt is owed to Linda Olson. She has served diligently and with imagination as a research assistant throughout the entire term of this project. She has helped gather the data, has helped analyze it, and has been the person chiefly responsible for the day-to-day organization of the mass of information we have collected.

We are grateful to Albert Crambert of the United States Office of Education for his personal help and advice up to 1974 and to Oliver Moles, of the National Institute of Education, who has helped us in the same way since. The research has been facilitated by NIMH Small grant #MH 18183, Office of Education grant #OEG-3-71-0122, and is currently supported by National Institute of Education grant #NIE-G-74-0029. In addition, final preparation of this book was facilitated by a Guggenheim fellowship awarded Doris Entwisle.

To the teachers and students of the schools participating in this work, and to the principals and other staff in these schools, we are more grateful than words can express. They have welcomed us, assisted us, counseled us, and encouraged us in myriad ways. We have derived enormous benefit from consulting with them. We regret that they must remain anonymous in order to protect confidentiality. We must say, however, that this research would have been impossible without their help; any contribution it makes reflects their efforts as well as our own. We acknowledge with appreciation the help given by Dr. George Gabriel and Dr. John Crew, who made the necessary administrative arrangements for conducting this research in Baltimore County and Baltimore City.

CHAPTER 1

Questions about Expectations

This book is about young children's academic expectations—how well first and second graders expect to do in school. Many people have conjectured that children's expectations for themselves and others' expectations for them are crucial in the process of academic development. Yet, to our knowledge, no one has ever studied precisely how such expectations develop.

The work reported here had its beginnings in early 1969. At that time one of us (D.R.E.), in collaboration with Murray Webster, undertook some field experiments to see if it was possible to raise children's expectations for their own performance at a simple task. The answer was "Yes." The experimental work continued along the same lines for several years (see Entwisle and Webster, 1974a, 1974b). These field experiments and some laboratory experiments by Murray Webster were given the theoretical context of "expectation states theory." (See Berger, Conner, and Fisek, 1974, for a comprehensive exposition of that theory; also see earlier theoretical statements of Berger, Zelditch and Anderson, 1966.)

A basic idea in the theory is that expectations depend on evaluations. If a child is told, for instance, that he is good at arithmetic, he develops ideas about himself (expectations) consistent with that evaluation.* These ideas lead him to behave in ways that make the evaluations come true. The child who believes he is good at arithmetic, for example, will be likely to try hard to do problems in arithmetic or to count his change carefully every time he buys something.

In the field experiments designed to raise children's expectations we were struck by how much variation there was in the expectations different children had at the start of the experiments. Some came to the experiments with high expectations, others came with low expectations. The experiments demonstrated beyond a doubt that it was possible to raise children's expectations in a setting much like that of a classroom, but as the experiments continued a much more pressing question emerged: What happens to children in the ordinary course of their lives that causes them to build high or low expectations for themselves? What happens day by day, from the time they start school, to shape their academic expectations? Short experiments have merit because they can answer specific small questions, but

---

*The masculine pronoun is used throughout to avoid the awkwardness of he/she constructions. In most instances "he" implies "he or she." (All the teachers in this study were female, however, so the female pronoun is used where appropriate.)

they also have drawbacks, since they span short periods of time and often preclude manipulating variables of key importance in real life—their ecological validity, in other words, is questionable. Our experiments could not, for example, deliberately lower children's expectations, nor could they assign children real marks and manipulate parents' expectations. Neither could we experiment over and over with the same children. Yet in life itself children repeatedly experience disappointments and frustrations that may lower their expectations. Their lives are crowded with events that sometimes bring joy and at other times bring tears of disappointment, depending on whether their performance confirms their expectations at that particular moment. One motive prompting the research reported in this book was a desire to compile the "natural history" of children's expectations.

This research was also provoked by perplexing questions of another kind. Why, with so many resources and with so much effort devoted to improving the school performance of low-achieving youngsters, are substantial improvements so rare? Why have interventions of various kinds borne so little fruit, especially for children who are poor and/or are members of minority groups? In fact, what exactly is it about social class that is linked to success in school? Although at first one might think that children from disadvantaged backgrounds would hold low opinions of themselves, recent research on this topic points toward the opposite conclusion (see Entwisle and Hayduk, 1977). Our work, the reader will see, makes us believe that disadvantaged or minority group children do not have low expectations. The work also gives some clues about how high expectations many *impede* performance.

Expectations are the pivotal concept of the book. The central questions are how school experience shapes children's early expectations for themselves in academic areas, and, in turn, how performance shapes expectations.

Parents, of course, almost from the moment children are born, have ideas about how well their children will do in school and, more generally, in life. The children themselves develop ideas about their own ability, not only from parents, but from peers, teachers, and others. Children's ideas about themselves and others' ideas about them may match actual performance, or the ideas may need revising. In either case we believe that the ideas children have about their own ability and the ideas others have about the children's ability exert powerful influences on the children's performances.

Thus, a child is not born with expectations. He builds them as he grows. Early experiences often foster high expectations. The child is in a period of rapid growth, and he compares his present self with his former self—performance is bound to be favorably evaluated. A child's first step, for instance, is followed in only a few days by his ability to walk. He is powerfully rewarded, not because he can walk better than other members of his family, but because he can walk. Similarly, he gets powerful rewards for developing other skills, like speech.

"Going to school" means the end of infancy and a slowing down of physiological maturation. It is a large step toward treasured independence, and children look forward to school as signalling a big change in status. What happens to a child's expectations for himself, though, when he goes to school? For one thing, the basis of rewards changes. As the child emerges from the protective circle of the family he finds himself rated according to how well he does *compared to others of his age,* not, as he was before, in terms only of how well he does with respect to his own past record. Also, people in school are attentive to the child's success at completely new and different activities. The basis for rating the child (or even who actually does the rating) may be obscure to the child. It turns out, of course, that the child is rated on his ability to please the teacher, impress his peers, and forecast others' responses to him, as well as on purely "cognitive" performance. He gets social feedback from many sources—teachers, principals, classmates—and the feedback may be difficult to interpret.

Once in school, furthermore, the child has no choice as to how much time he spends in various pursuits and, whether he finds the school's activities to his liking or not, his rewards depend on his attention to those activities. Success is no longer guaranteed. He cannot concentrate only on pursuits at which he excels. Even if he cannot tell one note from another he is urged to sing. Even if he is partially color-blind he must try to discriminate red from green. The lack of electives in first grade has profound significance; it means the child is helpless when it comes to guaranteeing himself success in an area.

Perhaps most important of all, once in school, the arena of behavior, and, therefore, the arena of evaluation, is greatly enlarged by the intrusion of achievement behaviors, reading, arithmetic, and the like. Children sense that serious evaluations are being made with respect to performance in these cognitive areas even though some children have had little or no experience before school with the kinds of behavior the cognitive activities require. Perhaps for the first time in some children's experience, there are serious elements of threat and the possibility of failure. Only one child can be "best" in reading when ranked with the rest of the class. With 30 children in a class, 29 are bound to suffer some loss of reward.

The early days of school plunge children into a confusing new environment of social comparison. The net residue of these comparisons, nevertheless, shapes the child's evaluation of himself, what we call his "expectations." We suspect that his expectations for the self are a crucial component in his development, for his views of himself will filter, color, and even determine his experiences. If he thinks he will do well he will be glad to try. If he thinks he will do poorly, however, he is apt to hang back and avoid doing the very things that will help learning. Low expectations, furthermore, are easily transmitted. Those who think poorly of themselves encourage others to adopt a pessimistic view of them. The person who holds himself in low esteem is apt to be held in low esteem by others.

Why Study Expectations?

Surprisingly, the way in which young children actually develop expectations for themselves has never been studied. There are several large-scale studies of expectations of older children, however, and these studies make the consequences of holding high or low expectations rather clear. In the famous Coleman (1966) report, minority-group children reported lower expectations for their ability to control events in their own lives than did majority-group children. It turned out that, the lower children's expectations for control, the poorer their academic records. Another study of junior-high and high-school students found that self-conceptions of ability predicted school performance better than IQ did (Brookover and co-workers, 1962, 1964, 1965, 1967).

Some smaller studies of younger children demonstrate that expectations have similar consequences for them. Lamy (1965) found that self-perceptions and IQ in kindergarten predicted reading achievement in first grade equally well, and Wattenberg and Clifford (1964) successfully predicted, from measures of self-concept procured from kindergartners, reading achievement two-and-one-half years later.

In none of these studies, however, is there direct evidence of how self-conceptions of ability are *initially* established, or evidence suggesting what leads some students to have high self-concepts and others low, the kind of question the present research tries to answer. It is surprising that no study has yet focused on how academic self-concepts are initially established. Lesser (1972) says there must be important effects when "the child exhibits his elementary skills like naming letters or numbers in the presence of someone who cares about him and receives attention and admiration," but how, in fact, a young child develops an image of himself as a competent and effective person or as an incompetent and ineffective person is shrouded in mystery. There is little research of any kind, it turns out, on children's expectations and aspirations in their earliest school years, especially research where the same children are studied over a period of time in a naturalistic setting. No doubt this is partly because it is difficult to study children before they are able to read and write.

What is to be gained from studying such children? We believe *early* school events may be crucial in forging the child's academic self-image. Both folk wisdom and scientific reports suggest that, by the end of third grade, *before* the age of competent reading and writing, children have developed fairly complex and stable self-images. How well children are doing academically at that age is a good long-term indicator of school performance. In Husèn's (1969) large cross-national study, for example, intelligence scores and teachers' rating in third grade were good predictors of subsequent educational careers, and Kraus's (1973) data, which describe children in New York City over a twenty-year period, showed the most significant measure to be the score obtained on the third-grade reading achievement test—there was a high correlation between this score and all subsequent reading, mathematics, and intelligence test scores.

Early events are clearly of overriding importance. Why? Because, once the cycle of self-fulfilling prophecy starts, expectations shape performance, then performance is evaluated, and the evaluations feed back to modify expectations—it may be a hard cycle to break. If a child's first report card rates him low on reading, his initial high expectations may be shattered or his low expectations confirmed. In the latter case, he may then make little effort and be given little opportunity to prove himself. An initial low mark may also lead a child's classmates to lower their opinion of him. Thus because of one event, in this case, a first mark that happened to be low, both the way a child treats himself and the way he is treated by his teacher and classmates may be altered. The kind of treatment he then comes to expect is altered and his performance changes to match. The low reading mark may have had no "real" basis. The mark may have been given because the teacher thought the child could do better or perhaps even because the teacher was required to issue a certain percentage of low marks. Such early events, however unrelated they might be to the child's actual potential, may nevertheless have profound implications for a child's academic career.

In this book we scrutinize early marks to see how they affect subsequent performance. We also examine how expectations children have before they get any marks at all change as the children are evaluated in the early school grades.

An Overview of the Research

This book focuses on the development of children's expectations for themselves from the time they start first grade. A handy way to conceptualize this development is in terms of the feedback model shown in figure 1.1. The child is visualized as existing in a social matrix where two-way

Figure 1.1

Schematic Expectation Model

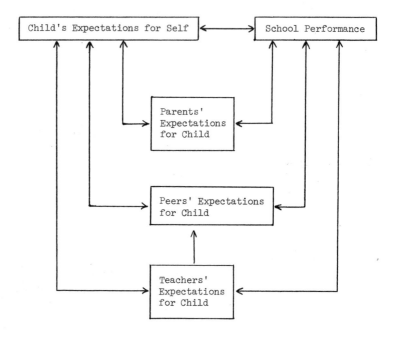

causation is the rule. Parents' expectations could shape children's expectations. Children's expectations could influence parents' expectations. Children's performance could change both the child's expectations and the
parents' expectations. The two-headed arrows in the model are meant to
indicate two-way effects.

Expectations and performances could be related to a number of other
factors not shown explicitly in figure 1.1, factors like the child's IQ, race,
sex, or other characteristics. Such considerations are important. The causal
forces portrayed in the diagram may differ for boys and for girls, or for
children from one social group as compared with those from another.
Causal forces may also have different impact according to whether the
child is bright or dull. A bright child, for example, may perceive readily
that he is doing better than his classmates or, because he is bright, he may
set higher standards for himself and not be satisfied with a mediocre per-

formance. The point is that, however IQ enters the picture, it probably affects feedback.

Some variables that could have important influences are not in the model (social-structural characteristics of classrooms, for example). Simpson (1975) found, in a cross-sectional study of third graders, that, in classrooms where mark assignments are frequent, where task-oriented grouping is infrequent, and where student autonomy is low (classrooms he defines as "unidimensional" rather than "multidimensional"), a wider range of students' academic self-concepts appears. The consistency between children's expectations in several different marking areas was not related to unidimensionality and, furthermore, there were no racial differences in the children's own expectations for either type of classroom. This type of classroom, however, did foster racial differences in both teachers' and peers' ratings. We have not isolated classroom effects in our research except when studying the effects of teacher race for mixed-race classrooms; thus we side-stepped a whole genre of potentially interesting research questions.

Our strategy in this book is one of trying to answer a series of specific questions about children's expectations, questions suggested by the model and by related considerations. Some major questions are:

(1) What academic expectations do children hold for themselves when they start school?

(2) How do the children's early performances compare to these expectations?

(3) How do children's expectations affect early school performance?

(4) How are expectations altered as a consequence of assigned marks?

(5) How important are significant others, especially parents, in the development of young children's expectations?

(6) How do factors such as sex, IQ, race, and social class impinge on both expectations and performance and on the relation between the two?

These questions only hint at the list that could be drawn up and cannot be answered as fully as they deserve to be. We can answer the simpler questions with some degree of certainty and cite some provocative findings that bear on the more complex questions. As with any research in a largely uncharted domain, further questions emerged out of the research as it progressed.

CONCEPTUAL GROUNDWORK FOR THE DESIGN AND ANALYSIS

The best way for the reader to conceptualize this research is by the unit of analysis. The unit of analysis is the schoolchild nested in a group of significant others: his parents, his peers, his teachers. But there could be many such models, because the child's social group is nested in a neighborhood and/or school. One can thus visualize a *set* of feedback models that differ from one another on the basis of the race, sex, or social class of the child. By focusing on the articulation of the child with his group and on the position of that group within society, we trace the way in which social factors and processes are translated into the expectations children hold, and the way children's expectations, in turn, affect their performance.

The research is longitudinal. It measures the same set of variables at several time points (see figure 1.2). The child's expectations for himself and other measures are secured repeatedly from a time before the child receives a first report card to the end of the second grade in some cases.

The obvious advantage of longitudinal data for individuals is that it does away with the confounding of causal explanations inherently present in cross-sectional data or in aggregated data. An average gain can imply many different kinds of performance at an individual level. A point that has received much attention in the development literature and is cogent here, however, is that longitudinal data need to be carefully studied to separate (1) effects of age, (2) effects of cohort,* and (3) effects of time of sampling. An example will make this clear. A child who is five years old in 1970 is obviously different from a child of six in 1970 because of attained age, but also because the five year old is drawn from a 1965 birth cohort and the six year old is a member of a 1964 birth cohort. Data on five- and six-year-old children taken in 1970 may differ from data on five and six year olds procured in 1971 due to systematic differences in events occurring in the preceding years, like a rise or a decline in the economy. Conditions of study in 1971 might, therefore, differ as a result of two factors, first, sampling differences and, second, specific events intervening between 1970 and 1971 that differ from events between 1969 and 1970 (i.e., differences in immediate historical experiences). As a consequence, effects of age, cohort, and time of sampling all need specification.

Fortunately, in the present research, the time span for gathering data is relatively short and the same schools are used to locate successive cohorts. These facts provide the basis for our assumption that, for any one cohort, differences between observations of first and second graders are largely age or experience differences rather than historical differences stemming from time of sampling. By looking at each cohort separately and neglecting time

---

*"Cohort" is a term used by demographers and means a group of persons who are studied beginning at some particular time. The "birth cohort of 1940 in the United States" would mean all persons born in the United States in 1940. In the present research "cohort" means all the first-grade children starting in a particular school in a particular year.

Figure 1.2

Observation Periods

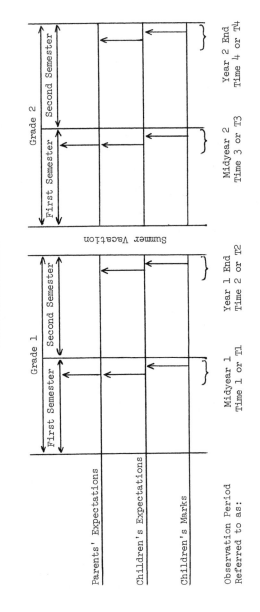

Notes:

1) an "↑" indicates observations were made on this variable (set) at the indicated time.

2) "Time 1" (etc.) refer to the Grade 1 – Semester 1 (etc.) observations made on a cohort no matter when the cohort was actually observed in terms of years.

of sampling differences—looking, for example, at first graders in the same school in 1971 and in 1972—to see if samples of the same attained age differ, we can estimate the size of cohort differences. As the reader will see, cohort differences, insofar as they are available (for one school only), appear to be small. This fortunate state of affairs allows cohorts to be combined, and, neglecting time of sampling on a priori grounds, we then attribute any observed changes to differences in age or maturation.

Like many sociological studies, this work studies contextual variables and tries to impose a causal paradigm. Children's expectations at the end of first grade, for example, are studied in the context of the child's expectations earlier that year, his parents' expectations, and previous marks received, among other things. The number of cases involved (so far 150 at the maximum), the nature of the measurement (often a four-point discrete scale), and the absence of a fully specified model abrogate a complete definitive analysis at this stage. In this book repeated cross tabulations are carried out where *change* in one variable is tabulated against earlier differences in other variables to locate causal relations. Such analyses can examine, for example, whether children with low initial expectations revise their expectations upward after receiving marks higher than they expected, or whether marks and expectations change simultaneously so as to increase the agreement between them from one time point to the next. Or, to take another example, if some parents expect boys to do poorly in reading, we can examine how the expectations of both parents and boys are affected by the marks the boys receive. Many more analyses were explored than are presented in this book. In cases where results were null, only the outcomes of analyses will be given. Rather complete data will be given for discussion of the most basic issues.

In summation, we say that the present research attempts to look at the *course of development* of children's expectations—their academic self-images—in several areas. The aim is to see how performance feedback shapes and is shaped by the academic self-image, and how feedback from particular persons shapes the image. The social context is involved in two ways, first, as the set of particular significant others, and, second, as the social class or racial mix of the child's surroundings.

CHAPTER 2

Setting, Procedures, and Analysis

This report covers two school years for one cohort of middle-class children (S-1), one year for another cohort of middle-class children (S-2), and one year for a cohort of working-class children (L-1). As mentioned, the three cohorts of children have been followed from the time they began first grade. One of the cohorts drawn from the white middle-class suburban school (S-1) began first grade in 1971; the other, S-2, began first grade in 1972. The third cohort was drawn from an integrated (60 percent black) urban working-class school and began first grade in 1972. Insofar as possible, similar data and information were obtained for all three cohorts.

At times data for the middle-class school are aggregated by combining data on the two successive first-grade classes (S-1 and S-2). This aggregation allows fairly extensive analyses. Data for the working-class school are more restricted because they are based on a single cohort of first graders (L-1). All black-white comparisons stem from the L-1 cohort.

Setting and Procedures

SCHOOL DIFFERENCES

Several factors besides social class and race account for differences between the two schools from which cohorts were drawn. These factors are confounded with class differences, though, so the reader must be cautious in attributing effects to differences in social class or to segregation/integration alone. The schools were chosen as "typical" examples of middle-class white and integrated working-class schools, but, obviously, the representativeness of these schools is a matter for personal judgment.

An estimate of population differences in the two communities served by the schools was obtained from the 1970 census (table 2.1).* The working-class school serves most of four census tracts, the middle-class school serves most of three. The middle-class school is white segregated, its regular staff is white with one or two exceptions, and its classrooms have no aides. It is located in a quiet residential neighborhood of well-landscaped individual homes worth $60,000 or more at 1976 prices. The

*Also see Appendix A.

Table 2.1

1970 Community Census Statistics for the Suburban Middle-Class and Urban Working-Class Schools

Tract Number	Middle-Class School [a]				Working-Class School [a]				
	1	2	3	Ave.	1	2	3	4	Ave.
Median Years of School Completed by Head of Household	12.4	13.6	12.9	13.0	10.2	8.4	10.2	8.5	9.4
Mean Income	$13,294	$24,101	$17,036	$18,143	$8,573	$6,487	$8,074	$8,165	$7,825
Median Value Owner-Occupied Houses	$19,200	$30,600	$28,200	$26,000	$6,300	$6,000	$10,200	$5,800	$7,075
Percentage Black	0.0%	0.0%	0.2%	0.1%	63.7%	92.4%	7.3%	8.1%	18.5%
Percentage of All Families with Income Below Poverty Level	3.2%	1.1%	2.0%	2.1%	20.2%	36.2%	15.8%	14.2%	21.6%

[a] The use of labels "middle-class" and "working-class" is for convenience. In particular, "working-class" covers a wide range of possibilities here, from father-absent families whose children qualify for free lunches to families with stable and substantial incomes.

school building, recently enlarged and renovated, has a large library, a cafeteria where hot food is prepared at noon, and a large playground.

The working-class school has an integrated (roughly fifty-fifty) staff and an aide in every kindergarten and first-grade class. The school is set on a busy street corner in an urban residential area where traffic is heavy. Many of the nearby row houses, worth from $6,000 to $20,000, depending on exact location and internal condition, have been turned into apartments for three or more families. Parts of the school building were erected before the turn of the century; the school has its own playground, a large gymnasium, and a large library. Hot lunches are delivered daily to the school. Many children in this school have family incomes low enough to qualify for free lunches. The school has the services of several "resource teachers" who work at the school full-time and help classroom teachers with reading instruction.

The two schools are close to the same size, with three or four first-grade classes apiece, depending on total enrollment. Staff quality in both schools is high. Formal credentials of the staff in the working-class school may be superior to those of the middle-class school staff. In both schools there are many teachers with several years' service. Classroom size is about the same in the two schools.

Both schools have kindergartens with half-day sessions attended by most of the children who later enter first grade. Little study of these kindergartens has been made so far, but one difference between schools important for this research is that the working-class school gives report cards to kindergartners. We attempted to query kindergartners there about their expectations for report cards but were unable to procure responses we felt were valid. In many cases the child would not respond at all; in other cases it was clear the child did not understand what we were asking him to do. Thus the meaning of "first report card" may not be exactly the same in both schools. There is no way at present to evaluate any effects the kindergarten report cards may have had.

The time chart given earlier in figure 1.2, shows the sequence and timing of several measures taken repeatedly over a two-year time span. The measures identified on the time chart are described in the next section.

THE CHILDREN'S EXPECTATION MEASURE

To provide a measure of the child's expectations, individual children were asked to guess what their next report card would look like, to guess what they would get in reading . . . in arithmetic . . . and in conduct. For the initial measuring of expectations, a large, brightly-colored plastic sheet (approximately two feet by three feet) was prepared (see figure 2.1) with

Figure 2.1

Stylized Report Card Replica

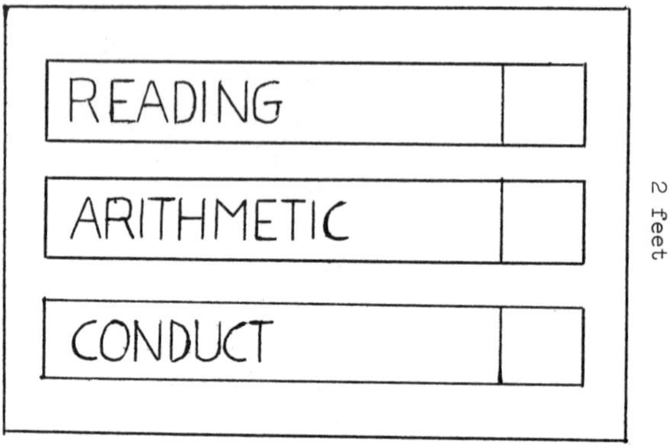

3 feet

titles of school subjects (reading, arithmetic, conduct) and squares for entering marks, like on a report card. This sheet was spread out on a table or, sometimes, on the floor. Next to the sheet were piles of cardboard squares with large numerals (1, 2, 3, 4) or letters (A, B, C, D) inked on them.

Children were interviewed individually outside their classroom and were told, "We are going to play a game—guessing what you will get on your report card." Before "playing the game," the child was asked if he knew what a report card was, what the numerals or letters meant, and what "reading," "arithmetic," and "conduct" meant. Discussion continued until the interviewer felt the child understood what school report cards signified and how marks were coded.* Only then was the child asked to show what he guessed he would get in reading by picking a numeral from the pile of numerals and placing it in the square next to "reading." He was similarly asked to pick numerals to represent his guesses for arithmetic and conduct. (Letters were used in place of numerals when it was appropriate.) As the child made guesses the interviewer unobstrusively recorded the

_____

*At a later time a separate interview was conducted with each child by a different interviewer. These interviews verified the child's understanding of marks and the marking systems without reference to the guessing task. The independent verification is discussed in connection with results.

marks on a 3" × 5" card. The cards were kept out of sight; it is doubtful that any of the children were aware their guesses were being recorded.

Report cards are issued three times in first grade and four times in second grade. Initial interviews for measuring expectations in reading, arithmetic, and conduct were held just before the child received his first report card in first grade. A second interview was used to obtain the child's expectations just prior to the issuance of the year-end report card for grade one. In second grade, children's expectations were obtained just before report cards were issued for the second and fourth times. Thus expectations were recorded prior to the midyear and year-end report cards in both grades, but the first-grade midyear report card was also these children's *first* report card.

The expectation measure appears to have a fair degree of validity and reliability. A reliability check run on a small sample of first graders with one week between test and retest indicated a high degree of concordance between expectations elicited on the two occasions ($r = 0.76$).

PEER RATING

Two methods were used to procure peer ratings of children within their own classroom. The first used a multiple-choosing procedure that forced a child to pick six children on two occasions (twelve choices altogether) in such a way that choices would be widely distributed among the members of a classroom. Ranks were normalized to fall at equal intervals between zero (high popularity) and one (low popularity), and to standardize for classroom size. The multiple-choosing procedure was used only with S-1 in first grade.

Beginning in 1972 another peer rating procedure was used with all classrooms (S-1 in second grade, S-2 in first grade, and L-1 in first grade). A boy and a girl in each class were designated as captains. Captains took turns choosing their classmates to be members of their team in order to "play a reading game." As the captains took turns choosing children to be on their teams, a research assistant noted the order in which children were chosen. This procedure resulted in two separate rankings, one made for each captain's team, with the captain of each team being assigned the highest rank. Often, but not always, the teams chosen were homogeneous by sex. The ranks by class were converted into scores between zero and one so as to be comparable to the scores obtained by the multiple-choosing procedure and, also, of course, to normalize them with respect to classroom size.

The peer rating measurement was carried out once per school year (at some time in the second semester) per cohort. It produced a within-room popularity score. Both the way the choosing occurred and the high correspondence observed for the first half-dozen children chosen for each team when the choosing was repeated on a few occasions (peer ranking performed by one working-class group of 20 children on two occasions one week apart, for example, produced a correlation between rankings of 0.73) suggest that there is a fairly clear, stable ordering for at least the top half (on the basis of popularity) of the class. For the bottom half the ordering among individuals appears less stable.

DATA FROM SCHOOL RECORDS: SEX, RACE, IQ, ABSENCES, STANDARDIZED ACHIEVEMENT TEST SCORES, AND TEACHERS' MARKS

All these data were procured from pupil folders and can best be described in detail along with the presentation of results.

In both schools teachers assigned marks in a wide variety of subjects. (See figures 2.2 and 2.3 for replicas of report cards in use in the middle-class and working-class schools. Both schools have since changed their methods of reporting marks.) The reader should note that the teachers' bases for assigning marks, according to the report card definition, were quite different in the two schools. In the middle-class school the teacher attempted to mark the child in relation to his own ability. In the working-class school the teacher attempted to mark the child in relation to grade norms.

SELF-ESTEEM

Self-esteem was measured on a scale especially developed for use with young children (Dickstein, 1972) that provides separate scales for boys and girls. Each scale contains three factors. These factor scores have been kept separate for the analysis and have thus yielded three different indicators of self-esteem for each sex. The items (abbreviated) are shown here for each factor, separately by sex:

	Boys	
I	II	III
polite	sports	arithmetic
cooperative	strong	good student
obeying rules	playing ball	learns new things quickly
kind	many friends	
helpful	gymnastics	
honest	running	
good student	right weight	
	able to look after others	

	Girls	
I	II	III
can look after others	sports	good-looking
can take care of herself	strong	many friends
polite	gymnastics	right weight
good student	playing ball	good student
learns new things quickly	running	polite
writing	dancing	
arithmetic		
honest		

For mnemonic reasons we label these respective factors as the boy scout, athlete, and scholar factors for the boys, and the achiever, athlete, and social-butterfly factors for the girls.

This paper and pencil test, given during the second semester of each year, produced scores based on how the children rated themselves on the various items. Three separate self-esteem scores were computed for each child by summing the appropriate response scores and calculating a within-year (within-cohort) standard score for each of the three factors. The signs of the standard scores were reversed to provide a positive score for high self-esteem.

PARENTS' EXPECTATIONS AND QUESTIONNAIRE

Data from parents in the middle-class school were collected once each year, in many instances by a short interview when parents visited their child's classroom during American Education Week in late October. Parents not available for interviewing at that time were sent questionnaires by mail.

Parents in the working-class school were also interviewed at school when possible. The difficulties in securing the needed information from interviews of these parents at the school led us *not* to mail questionnaires to other parents. Rather, black adult female interviewers were dispatched to homes of black children, and white adult female interviewers to homes of white children. Refusal rates and other data are given with the results. Only one parent, usually the mother, was interviewed for each family.

The data procured from parents was, insofar as possible, identical for the two schools. The parents were asked to predict what their child would get on his next report card, and the interviewers recorded these guesses on sheets of paper containing replicas of part of the report card. Other information, indicating the content of parent-child interaction, family size, and the like, was also obtained, but is not included in this report.

Figure 2.2

Middle-Class School Report Card

R13955

----------- COUNTY PUBLIC SCHOOLS
PROGRESS REPORT

STUDENT _____

TEACHER _____

GRADE _____ SCHOOL YEAR 19____ 19____

SCHOOL _____

SUBJECTS	TERM 1		TERM 2		TERM 3		TERM 4	
	ACHIEVE	EFFORT	ACHIEVE	EFFORT	ACHIEVE	EFFORT	ACHIEVE	EFFORT
READING								
WORD ATTACK SKILLS								
COMPREHENSION SKILLS								
ARITHMETIC								
KNOWLEDGE OF NO. SYSTEM								
COMPUTATION								
PROBLEM SOLVING								
SPELLING								
BASIC WORD LIST								
OTHER WRITTEN WORK								
LANGUAGE								
WRITTEN EXPRESSION								
ORAL EXPRESSION								
SOCIAL STUDIES								
REFERENCE SKILLS								
BASIC UNDERSTANDING								

	TERM 1	TERM 2	TERM 3	TERM 4
HANDWRITING				
ART				
MUSIC				
PHYSICAL EDUCATION				
STUDY HABITS				
CONDUCT				

CODE: G = GOOD S = SATISFACTORY P = POOR

	TERM 1	TERM 2	TERM 3	TERM 4
TEACHER REQUESTS CONFERENCE				
IS BEING CONSIDERED FOR RETENTION				

JUNE 19 _____

PROMOTED TO GRADE _____

WILL WORK WITH GRADE _____

RETAINED IN GRADE _____

ASSIGNMENT SEPT. 19 _____

ROOM _____

ACHIEVEMENT CODE (BASED ON GRADE STANDARDS)

A - SUPERIOR
B - ABOVE AVERAGE
C - AVERAGE
D - LOW AVERAGE (LOWEST PASSING GRADE)
E - DID NOT ATTAIN MINIMUM GRADE STANDARDS
"N" - INDICATES IMPROVEMENT NEEDED IN A PARTICULAR SKILL

EFFORT CODE

1 - MAXIMUM
2 - HIGH AVERAGE
3 - AVERAGE
4 - LOW AVERAGE
5 - MINIMUM

BERCO 800 70

THIS IS YOUR RECORD. IT NEED NOT BE RETURNED TO SCHOOL

Figure 2.2 (Continued)

To the Parents:

This is the schools report to you on the progress of your child.

Reporting periods close on November 15, January 31, April 15, and at the end of the school year. Reports will be sent to you within a week of the close of each term. Your copy of the report need not be returned.

In the academic area your child will receive two marks - a letter grade (A, B, C, D, or E) for Achievement in relation to grade standards and a number (1, 2, 3, 4 or 5) to indicate Effort. "N" where shown indicates improvement needed in that particular skill. "D" is the lowest passing grade.

Note: Grade one pupils will receive no mark in spelling during the year.

The other areas, Handwriting, Art, Music, Physical Education, Study Habits and Conduct, are marked with a three point scale using G, S, and P as described.

A child being considered for retention at the end of the second or third term will receive a check (√) in the space provided.

A space has also been provided for the teacher to request a conference. Please contact the teacher and arrange an appointment if indicated. You are invited, however, to ask for a conference at any time.

Superintendent of Schools

Figure 2.3
Working-Class School Report Card

349 40 0151

----------PUBLIC SCHOOLS

REPORT OF

(LAST NAME FIRST)

SCHOOL NAME AND NO.

TEACHER

GRADE OR LEVEL_____SCHOOL YEAR ENDING JUNE 19___

ACHIEVEMENT CODE

A – OUTSTANDING   D – POOR
B – GOOD   U – UNSATISFACTORY
C – SATISFACTORY

EFFORT AND HABITS CODE

1 – GOOD
2 – SATISFACTORY
3 – UNSATISFACTORY

	NOVEMBER REPORT	MARCH REPORT	JUNE REPORT
READING			
BOOK LEVEL			
ENGLISH LANGUAGE ARTS			
HANDWRITING			
LISTENING			
SPEAKING			
SPELLING			
WRITTEN ENGLISH			
MATHEMATICS			
HEALTH AND SAFETY			
SCIENCE			
SOCIAL STUDIES			
ART			
MUSIC			
PHYSICAL EDUCATION			

	NOVEMBER REPORT	MARCH REPORT	JUNE REPORT
CONDUCT			
EFFORT			
HEALTH HABITS			
HOMEWORK			
SAFETY HABITS			
WORK HABITS			

TOTAL TIMES LATE TO DATE
TOTAL DAYS ABSENT TO DATE

TEACHER REQUESTS   DATE
A CONFERENCE   TIME

TEACHER COMMENTS ATTACHED

	YES	NO	YES	NO	YES	NO
PUPIL MAY NEED MORE TIME AT THIS LEVEL						

ASSIGNMENT NEXT YEAR

CONFERENCE SECTION

_____I SHALL BE ABLE TO KEEP THIS APPOINTMENT.

_____I SHALL NOT BE ABLE TO KEEP THIS APPOINTMENT.

I SHOULD LIKE TO HAVE A CONFERENCE WITH YOU ON

_____   _____OR._____
DATE   DATE   DATE

TEAR ALONG THE DOTTED LINE AND RETURN THE LOWER PORTION

PUPIL'S NAME_____ROOM NO.

_____I HAVE STUDIED THIS REPORT.

PARENT'S SIGNATURE

SCHOOL NAME AND NUMBER

Figure 2.3 (Continued)

A Few Helps in Understanding This Report

Your child's progress is reported in terms of his achievement in certain subject and habit areas. He is being measured in terms of his progress in reaching standards or levels that are considered appropriate for his age or years in school.

The letter "D" is used to show a barely satisfactory level of work. No parent or child should be satisfied with this grade. The child should strive to do work that is satisfactory or better.

Reading is a complex skill that involves the use of many types of materials. Some books show a grade level. Other materials do not.

The book level is indicated to let you know what book your child is handling in the classroom. These are the symbols used for readers:

PR — Material a child is using in getting ready to read

PP — Pre-primer material or first printed material in book form that is introduced to the child.

P — Primer material or material that gives many reading experiences before use of the first reader.

1 — First reader   } Publisher's grading of
2, 3, 4, 5, 6, 7, 8, etc. } a book

For further information about your child's progress in reading or in any other area, you are urged to talk with his teacher.

You may also send your comments to the principal of the school your child is attending or to the Elementary Division, ----------------------------------

INFORMATION FOR PARENTS

Your child's success is not only important to you and your child but also to all of us who work in the _____ Public Schools.

Three times during the school year, your child will bring home a report card. All you need to do for us is to cut off the lower portion, check that you have seen it, sign your name, and have your child return it to his teacher.

Look at the line Teacher Comments Attached. If the teacher has written yes, a special form will be stapled to the report card. If the teacher has written no, there will be no form attached to the report card.

You are encouraged to come in for a conference with your child's teacher. Each report form has a section where you may request a conference. Please use this section.

You are always welcome to come to school to talk about your child's progress.

Analysis

Data reduction was accomplished mainly through use of standard DATATEXT programs. Further analyses and tests were calculated as needed. Selected results and the accompanying analyses are presented in chapters 3, 4, and 5. In chapters 6 and 7 the implications of the findings and conclusions are presented. All marks and expectations are given in terms of digits from one to four, where one is high. The mark "A" was transformed to "1," "B" to "2," and so on, for both schools.

We used several different kinds of tests to assess differences or relationships in the data. Many of these tests led to use of a χ^2 statistic to evaluate the significance of an outcome, but the reader should not be misled into thinking that we used only the usual χ^2 tests for association in two-way tables. The tests answer various questions, including, among others: (1) Is there a significant match between one set of expectations and another, for example, between parents' expectations for reading and children's expectations for reading, or between children's expectations for reading and their expectations for arithmetic? (Matching.) (2) Does the distribution of marks awarded correspond to the distribution of marks parents expected? (Marginal homogeneity.) (3) For children whose marks changed, are changes more likely to be in an upward than downward direction? (Quasi-symmetry.) (4) In the case where there is no match between marks and expectations at one time, are there changes over time that tend to produce matching? (5) Are mark and expectation changes consistent or inconsistent with previous differences between marks and expectations?

Despite our hopes to the contrary, log linear models, models of the kind Goodman has proposed for use with categoric data (see Bishop, Fienberg, and Holland, 1975), turned out not to be suitable for our data. Readers interested in the technical details of why log linear models failed to be useful are referred to Appendix B to this chapter.

Appendix A

Since this manuscript was begun, the Maryland State Department of Education published the *Maryland Accountability Program Report, School Year 1973–74*. This report gives data for the middle-class and working-class schools of the present study using updated ESEA Title I statistics from 1970 census data. Some of the report data can be usefully compared with data in table 2.1.

Children in third grade in 1973–74 were tested in all Maryland schools

Table A2.1

Maryland Accountability Program Report Statistics

	School Enroll- ment	Pupil Staff Ratio	Average Daily Attend- ance (%)	Average Experience of Teachers (Years)	Staff Masters Degree or Above (%)	Percentage Disad- vantaged	Mother's Median Education	Median Family Income
Middle-Class School	659	20.7	97.1	10.1	28.3	2.2	12.5	$14,869
Working-Class School	784	24.9	88.8	11.1	28.6	29.3	10.0	$7,435

between 15 April and 15 May 1974. Cohort S-1 are the third graders included in the report. The working-class third graders in the report are the class one year ahead of cohort L-1. Nevertheless, we summarize in table A2.1 data of interest in the report for both schools involved in the data reported in this book.

Table 2.1 was based on 1970 census tract data (with some adjustments due to the lack of exact correspondence between census tract and school district boundaries). The mean income of middle-class children's families reported in table 2.1 is overestimated compared to table A2.1, and the percentage "disadvantaged" is somewhat underestimated compared to the report data. (Here, 29.3% of the working-class families are reported as disadvantaged, compared to the 21.6% of the families having "income below poverty level" as reported in table 2.1.) We may take the report data as being more accurate in both these regards. The pupil-staff ratio is misleading, however, because every first-grade classroom in the working-class school had a full-time aide as well as a teacher. The middle-class school had no aides. All the other information presented in table A2.1 agrees favorably with our previous description of these schools.

Appendix B

A log linear model fits an equation with several terms to a discrete data matrix (see Bishop, Fienberg, and Holland, 1975). Various models with differing numbers of terms can be tried; for example, it might be possible to fit a two-dimensional table (requiring four terms at most) with only a three-term model. How good the fit was would be assessed by comparing χ^2 values for the fitted (three-term) and saturated (four-term) models. To take this example further, if a three-term model did fit, the conclusion would be that there was no interaction between the two variables used to form the two-dimensional table. If the model did not fit, we would conclude there was an interaction. But this can be an uninformative answer unless we look at the fit cell-by-cell and see where the interaction is arising.

In our data we often have substantive reasons for being interested in interactions of a special type—those manifested by overrepresentation on a diagonal, for example. To say that a large contribution to the χ^2 computed for fit of a log linear model comes from the diagonal cells seems considerably more awkward than to say that the basic question is one of matching. The matching test, derived by estimating the mean and variance for particular multinomial distributions, asks specifically if an entire array of cells (major or minor diagonal) is large or not and sets confidence limits on the expected value of the match. Although such questions can be approached from the standpoint of log linear models, the approach is far from straightforward. Therefore, we used the test described by Bush and Mosteller (1954) to answer matching questions.

Some of the tests that we used turn out to be exactly the same tests that would be derived as a consequence of using a log linear approach. (See chapter 8 of Bishop, Fienberg, and Holland, 1975.) We could have said, for example, that in places where we tested for symmetry on either side of a main diagonal we were going to fold the table along the diagonal, ignore the diagonal, and then see whether a log linear model with four terms ($u_.$, $u_{1(i)}$, $u_{2(j)}$, $u_{12(ij)}$) fits this three-dimensional table (two layers of a triangular table containing several structural zeros) fabricated from our original two-dimensional table. This technique combines a cell-by-cell test and an over-all frequency test of symmetry. We were not very interested, however, in a cell-by-cell test; rather, we wanted an overall frequency test. We therefore tested symmetry in several places using formulas for an overall test (see Bishop, Fienberg, and Holland, p. 285). The overall test of symmetry can be described as fitting a log linear model with the four previous terms plus $u_{3(k)}$ to the table potentially generated by up to eight terms (the four listed above plus $u_{3(k)}$, $u_{13(ik)}$, $u_{23(jk)}$, $u_{123(ijk)}$). Such a description, however, seems excessive.

The number of observations available in the present data is a serious impediment to a log linear approach. In many cases we have 3×3 (nine-cell) or 4×4 (sixteen-cell) tables. We also have about one hundred cases as a working basis in most tables. This means that the analysis has to proceed two variables at a time. (A three-variable breakdown implies an average expected value of about three cases per cell even if we stick with only three categories per variable.) All our analyses would thereby be restricted to asking whether there was an interaction in a two-way table, followed by a cell-by-cell ransacking to see where the interaction was.

Also, most of the examples of log linear analysis in the literature employ dichotomous variables or, once in a while, trichotomies. With dichotomies, four variables lead to 16 cells, but, with our data, four variables lead to 256 cells. The number of variables, of course, is directly related to the structure of the model. Being limited mainly to two variables, we cannot ask very interesting structural questions via log linear models. We can, however, ask such questions by using intuition plus a test tailored to those questions.

In our analysis the judicious (and substantively meaningful) combination of variables to create other *single* variables (like the discrepance variable obtained by subtracting marks from expectations and other similar variables) provides a way around dimensionality problems created by a log linear approach. We ask specifically whether changes in marks follow discrepances of particular types. The log linear procedure would require three dimensions (marks at two times and expectations at one time) where primary interest attaches to the presence of a three-way interaction, but where we show there is no two-way interaction. In other words, we have evidence that the hierarchical assumption demanded by log linear models is violated. If marks and expectations are not related at time one—no interaction between variables one and two—then asking whether there is a change in this one-two interaction over time is equivalent to asking if there is a one-two-three interaction. But log linear models *must* be hierarchical— having a one-two-three interaction demands a one-two interaction by the structure of the model.

To repeat, we used several different specific tests to answer questions that occur frequently in these data: tests for symmetry, tests for marginal homogeneity, tests for matching, and tests for evaluating certain special kinds of change. Many of the tests employ a χ^2 statistic, but the questions being asked cover many topics besides the two-way association tested by an "ordinary" χ^2 test.

At this writing the difficulties and drawbacks associated with using log linear models on polytomous variables are not widely appreciated. There is the problem, already mentioned, of the size of the data base. With four dichotomous variables, a data matrix has 2^4 or 16 cells. With four four-category variables, the cells number 4^4 or 256, a 16-fold increase. More important conceptually, with dichotomous data each parameter in the saturated model has an isomorphic relation with the cell structure. In a 2×2 table the $u_{12(ij)}$ term is associated with a single degree of freedom, and, as terms are added to a model where all variables are dichotomous, there continues to be a single "new" data cell added for each parameter added to the model. In a 4×4 table the $u_{12(ij)}$ term has nine degrees of freedom, so adding this single parameter is linked to addition of nine "new" data cells. As the dimensionality of the table increases, there are many "new" cells added as each new parameter is added. In the case of dichotomous variables, the interpretation is straightforward. If a parameter is significant the investigator knows exactly what effect to point to in the data. In the case of polytomous variables, this isomorphism is lost, for a significant parameter means that one, several, or, perhaps, all of a particular set of cells exceed expectation. In most applications, including our own, such general answers (such imprecise models) have limited usefulness.

CHAPTER 3

Middle-Class Children in First Grade

The middle-class school from which two cohorts were drawn lies just north of the boundary of a large eastern city, in a well-established residential neighborhood. The school enrolls 600 to 700 children and there are three or four first-grade classrooms. The number of first-grade classes depends on yearly enrollment. Children who began first grade at this school in September 1971 (cohort S-1) have been followed, so far, through two school years. Children who started at the same school one year later, in September 1972 (cohort S-2), have been followed, so far, through one school year.

Data for children of both cohorts through their first grade are summarized in table 3.1. Results are discussed for both cohorts combined, except in the few instances when significant inter-cohort differences appear.

Middle-class children from this school are clearly optimistic about how well they will do when they start first grade, and a·year's experience in school does not decrease their optimism (table 3.1). Initial expectations for arithmetic are not quite as high as those for reading, but even in arithmetic almost half the children expect an A on their first report card. In every subject (reading, arithmetic, and conduct) the average expectation is for a B+ on the first report card, and expectations get even higher as the year goes on. Children's expectations in reading and conduct increased significantly, in fact, over the first-grade year (t = 2.60, p < .05; t = 3.60, p < .01, respectively), but these gains are modest in absolute terms (0.18 and 0.31 units respectively). Children's expectations in arithmetic increased over the year, also, but not to a significant degree (t = 1.74, p < .10).

Expectations were obtained from 86% of the first graders' parents (in 98% of cases from the mother). Parents have lower expectations than their children, averaging slightly above a B in all three areas. The difference between the average expectations of parents and children does not give an accurate notion of the actual differences, however, for the children's distributions are markedly skewed and have larger variances at midyear. In reading, for example, 56% of the children expect to receive the highest mark, whereas only 25% of parents are that optimistic. At the other ex-

Table 3.1

Means, Standard Deviations for Separate Cohorts and Sum of
Cohorts during First-Grade Year
Middle-Class School

	Grade 1, Cohort S-1			Grade 1, Cohort S-2			Grade 1, Combined Cohorts		
	N	Mean	S.D.	N	Mean	S.D.	N	Mean	S.D.
PMA I.Q.	91	115.44	10.14	92	111.61	11.55	183	113.51	11.01
Parent's Expectation--Midyear									
Reading	84	1.96	0.57	76	1.80	0.67	160	1.89	0.62
Arithmetic	84	1.83	0.60	76	2.04	0.74	160	1.93	0.67
Conduct	79	1.89	0.55	75	1.97	0.70	154	1.93	0.63
Child's Expectation--Midyear									
Reading	90	1.63	0.90	96	1.79	0.96	186	1.72	0.94
Arithmetic	90	1.66	0.90	96	1.94	0.79	186	1.80	0.86
Conduct	90	1.68	0.90	96	2.13	1.05	186	1.91	1.00
Child's Expectation--Year-End									
Reading	90	1.42	0.60	94	1.65	0.60	184	1.54	0.61
Arithmetic	90	1.64	0.81	94	1.75	0.75	184	1.70	0.78
Conduct	90	1.49	0.72	94	1.71	0.73	184	1.60	0.73
Child's Mark--Midyear									
Reading	85	1.77	0.65	93	1.77	0.63	178	1.77	0.64
Arithmetic	85	1.82	0.49	93	2.01	0.62	178	1.92	0.57
Conduct	85	1.75	0.75	93	1.96	0.67	178	1.86	0.72
Child's Mark--Year-End									
Reading	86	1.69	0.76	94	1.77	0.59	180	1.73	0.68
Arithmetic	86	1.66	0.59	94	1.77	0.66	180	1.71	0.63
Conduct	86	1.88	0.83	94	1.76	0.67	180	1.82	0.75

Table 3.1 (Continued)

Summary of Changes over School Year

	Grade 1, Cohort S-1			Grade 1, Cohort S-2			Grade 1, Combined Cohorts		
	N	Mean	S.D.	N	Mean	S.D.	N	Mean	S.D.
Mark Change (Midyear Mark minus Year-End Mark)									
Reading	78	0.10	0.70	93	0.01	0.62	171	0.05	0.65
Arithmetic	78	0.19	0.56	93	0.25	0.64	171	0.22	0.60
Conduct	78	-0.04	0.63	93	0.20	0.60	171	0.09	0.63
Expectation Change (Midyear Expectation minus Year-End Expectation)									
Reading	85	0.24	0.88	89	0.18	1.14	174	0.21	1.02
Arithmetic	85	0.00	1.14	89	0.23	0.84	174	0.12	1.00
Conduct	85	0.21	1.03	89	0.47	1.19	174	0.35	1.12
Child's Midyear Mark-Expectation Discrepancy (Midyear Mark minus Midyear Expectation)									
Reading	82	0.18	1.07	90	-0.03	1.08	172	0.07	1.07
Arithmetic	82	0.18	0.97	90	0.04	0.91	172	0.11	0.94
Conduct	82	0.10	1.06	90	-0.18	1.20	172	-0.05	1.14
Child's Year-End Mark-Expectation Discrepancy (Year-End Mark minus Year-End Expectation)									
Reading	84	0.27	0.87	91	0.11	0.71	175	0.19	0.79
Arithmetic	84	0.02	0.88	91	0.02	0.86	175	0.02	0.86
Conduct	84	0.37	0.92	91	0.03	0.90	175	0.19	0.92

treme, ten children (6.5%) expect to get the poorest mark, whereas only two parents (1.3%) forecast such a low mark.

On the average, teachers' marks in reading fell between what parents and children expected on every occasion.* Teachers, in general, awarded high marks—no D's were given, and from 85% to 90% A's and B's were assigned overall. The relative number of A's and B's, however, differed considerably from one area to another. About equal numbers of A's and B's are given in conduct, whereas more B's than A's were given in both reading and arithmetic. In all three areas, midyear and year-end marks matched significantly more than chance would predict—there was considerable stability in marks over the year.

The Relation of IQ to Expectations and Marks

The average IQ in the middle-class school (table 3.2), measured by the Primary Mental Abilities Test, is somewhat above average (114) with a standard deviation of 11.

Correlations of marks with IQ (table 3.2) are surprisingly small, and indicate the teachers are reasonably successful in implementing the school policy of marking the children in terms of their own ability. In cohort S-2 the relationships are stronger and more consistent than in cohort S-1. Why there are differences in IQ-mark correlations between cohorts is not clear. The same tests were used with both cohorts and two of three teachers were the same over both years.

The correlations between IQ and children's expectation level are generally negligible, suggesting that their expectations primarily reflect factors other than their own ability. In view of this, it is surprising to find strong and consistent correlations between IQ and parents' expectations. In every instance but one the correlations are highly significant, and, furthermore, for reading and arithmetic the correlations are sizeable, -0.443 and -0.499, respectively.

The correlations between parents' expectations and IQ provide a partial answer to the interesting question of how parents form their expectations. Two tendencies could be at work: (1) Parents may base their initial expectations for their child upon their recall of their own school perfor-

---

*A word is needed about how marks are assigned. At the first marking period (around the end of November) first graders do not receive a report card. They receive their first report card at the end of the first semester (around February 1). The card says: "This report is designed to measure the progress of your child in terms of his own maturity and ability." Thus children are supposed to be judged in terms of what they are capable of doing. Performance in this school is assessed in a way that attempts to partial out IQ.

Table 3.2

Correlations between IQ (PMA) and Other Measures
Middle-Class School, First Grade

	Cohort S-1		Cohort S-2		Combined Cohorts	
	Mean = 115.44		Mean = 111.61		Mean = 113.51	
	S.D. = 10.14		S.D. = 11.55		S.D. = 11.01	
	N	r	N	r	N	r
Parent's Expectation--Midyear						
Reading	81	-0.292**	72	-0.617**	153	-0.443**
Arithmetic	81	-0.429**	72	-0.525**	153	-0.499**
Conduct	76	-0.069	71	-0.353**	147	-0.227**
Child's Expectation--Midyear						
Reading	87	-0.172	88	-0.034	175	-0.109
Arithmetic	87	-0.065	88	-0.199	175	-0.163*
Conduct	87	0.063	88	0.034	175	0.002
Child's Expectation--Year-End						
Reading	85	-0.127	89	0.029	174	-0.076
Arithmetic	85	-0.026	89	-0.054	174	-0.053
Conduct	85	-0.070	89	0.016	174	-0.044
Child's Mark--Midyear						
Reading	82	-0.224*	89	-0.045	171	-0.123
Arithmetic	82	0.022	89	-0.298**	171	-0.219**
Conduct	82	-0.109	89	0.038	171	-0.055
Child's Mark--Year-End						
Reading	82	-0.099	90	-0.347**	172	-0.221**
Arithmetic	82	-0.008	90	-0.479**	172	-0.293**
Conduct	82	-0.043	90	-0.060	172	-0.030

* = significant at the .05 level.
** = significant at the .01 level.

mance. Above-average-IQ parents are likely both to have memories of doing well in school and to have produced offspring who also have above-average IQ's. The opposite would hold true for parents of below-average IQ. (2) Alternatively and more plausibly, parents' expectations for school marks and for performance on IQ tests may really be very similar expectations. A parent may perceive a child to be "bright" or "dull" and use this assessment in forming expectations for all kinds of academic pursuits. Middle-class parents are probably good at estimating their children's intellectual ability. We know, for example, that other adults (teachers) can guess children's IQ's rather accurately on the basis of classroom performance (Jensen, 1973), and of course many of the cues used by teachers are even more readily available to parents.

IQ, then, is not a good predictor of either children's marks or children's expectations in the middle-class school, but is impressively related to parents' expectations. IQ is a very important determinant of parental expectations, although exactly how the relation arises needs study. Parents are not told their child's IQ prior to the time they give their expectations. In a later section the relation between parents' and children's expectations will be explored.

Correspondence between Expectations and Marks

The correspondence between children's guesses for what their first marks will be and the marks they actually receive in all three areas fall within a range attributable to chance. (See Mosteller and Bush, 1954, pp. 310 ff., for the test procedures used.) A high percentage of children expect A's (55% expect A's in reading, for example), and some (6%) expect failure. Actually, no one fails.

By the end of the first grade, middle-class children improve slightly in their ability to forecast marks accurately. For reading, 53% of children ($z = 2.82$, $p < .01$) are correct, while, for arithmetic and conduct, the results still do not attain conventional significance levels (46%, $z = 1.65$, $p < .10$ and 43%, $z = 1.71$, $p < .10$, respectively).

Average expectations are too high to start with, yet the level of children's expectations in all three areas increases over the first-grade year. What could lead to this increase? Why should expectations increase when they outstrip both the children's level of attainment and, their parents' expectations? Much of what follows addresses this question by looking at changes in expectations in relation to prior marks, in relation to parent expectations, and in relation to other variables like sex and IQ.

The simplest question to ask is how much consistency there is between what a child expects at midyear and at the end of the year. About 48% of children hold the same expectations for reading at the end of the year as in the middle (table 3.4). This amount of persistence exceeds what would be expected by chance ($z = 2.10$, $p < .05$). In arithmetic the picture of persistence is similar—49% have the same expectations at the two times. In conduct, however, 40% voice the same expectations on the two occasions, not a significant amount of persistence. In all three areas the

Table 3.3

Joint Distribution of Middle-Class Children's Expectations and Marks, First Report Card

(Percentages, N = 172)

Mark, Midyear

		Reading				Arithmetic				Conduct				
		1	2	3	Total	1	2	3	Total	1	2	3	4	Total
Expectation, Midyear	1	17.4	32.0	5.8	55.2	9.9	30.8	2.9	43.6	19.2	20.3	6.4	0.6	46.5
	2	13.4	12.2	1.2	26.8	8.1	23.8	5.2	37.2	8.1	12.2	5.2	0.0	25.6
	3	1.7	7.6	2.3	11.6	2.3	10.5	1.7	14.5	4.7	11.0	3.5	0.0	19.2
	4	1.7	3.5	1.2	6.4	0.0	2.9	1.7	4.7	1.2	5.8	1.2	0.6	8.7
	Total	34.3	55.2	10.5	100.0	20.3	68.0	11.6	100.0	33.1	49.4	16.3	1.2	100.0

Table 3.4

Joint Distribution of Middle-Class Children's Expectations at Midyear and Year-End, First Grade

(Percentages, N = 172)

Expectation, Year-End

		Reading					Arithmetic					Conduct				
		1	2	3	4	Total	1	2	3	4	Total	1	2	3	4	Total
Expectation, Midyear	1	32.8	19.0	2.3	0.0	54.0	26.4	14.4	1.7	1.1	43.7	27.6	14.4	3.4	0.0	45.4
	2	13.2	13.2	0.0	0.0	26.4	12.1	19.5	4.0	0.6	36.2	15.5	6.9	2.9	0.0	25.3
	3	2.3	8.6	1.1	0.0	12.1	6.3	6.3	2.9	0.6	16.1	7.5	8.0	4.6	0.0	20.1
	4	4.6	1.7	0.6	0.6	7.5	1.7	0.6	1.1	0.6	4.0	4.0	3.4	1.1	0.6	9.2
	Total	52.9	42.5	4.0	0.6	100.0	46.6	40.8	9.8	2.9	100.0	54.6	32.8	12.1	0.6	100.0

upward movement is especially noticeable for children with low expectations at midyear (C's and D's).

For children whose expectations are B or C and for whom movement, therefore, could occur either up or down, no downward movement occurs for reading and little occurs for either arithmetic or conduct. Thus, using only data not subject to floor or ceiling effects, the upward thrust appears strong. Large upward changes in expectations are more likely than large downward changes despite the fact that there are many more children for whom large downward changes are possible. These trends will be discussed again when discrepances between marks and expectations are discussed.

In principle, marks may be assigned independently in all three areas on a range from A (high) to D (low), but the distributions of assigned marks are far from uniform. First, teachers' marking ranges were restricted; no D's were given in either arithmetic or reading at the middle of first grade, and only one D (in arithmetic) was given at year-end. Second, starting right from the time of first marking, the marks children receive in the different areas display a significant and consistent tendency to be the same: there is significant matching among marks given in all three subjects for both semesters.

Teachers, through their marking practices, thus signify that performance levels in reading and arithmetic are correlated. Children, however, do not anticipate this association. Children who think they will do well in reading on the first report card are apt not to think they will do well in arithmetic. Before the first report card, matches between children's expectations in the two areas occur in only 25% of the cases when, by chance, 36% matches would be predicted. This undermatching between initial reading and arithmetic expectations is highly significant ($z = 3.29$, $p < .01$) and, at the end of first grade, is still present ($z = 2.60$, $p < .01$) despite the similar marks given by teachers in the two areas on two prior report cards.

In sum, these middle-class children appear to start school with very high expectations overall, but particularly in reading. Two other important observations emerge. First, there is significant undermatching between expectations in reading and arithmetic. The children are anticipating that they will do better in one subject than in another. This phenomenon is one the reader should note carefully, for it appears in every cohort and is in direct opposition to teachers' marking practices. We take it as strong evidence of the construct validity of our measure of children's expectations because it does appear consistently and is counter to other trends. The second observation is that the inability of children to predict their marks has only partially disappeared by the end of first grade. About half the children can correctly predict their reading marks but their predictions for arithmetic and conduct remain at chance levels.

The Effects of Feedback

Much of the foregoing analysis examining correspondence between expectations and marks points toward ascertaining whether causal relations exist between children's performance and their expectations. What effects do first marks have on later expectations? Several related questions have been investigated in analyses too detailed to present here. In prefacing a little of what unfolds in this section, though, we can say that by far the strongest predictor of either marks or expectations is the *discrepance* between expectations and marks. That is, if a child does better or worse than he expects, this discrepance, rather than either the absolute level of his expectations or of his actual mark, is what exerts an impact.

Most of the data on reading, arithmetic, and conduct support the statement that children of all ability levels formulate their expectations in the same way before the first report card is received. The logic and style of analysis behind this statement is as follows. If children of all ability levels formed their expectations in a similar way, and if the mechanism they used for forming their expectations was independent of how their teachers rated their performance, one would expect children of all ability levels to display the same distribution of expectations. This model may be contrasted with one in which children do incorporate realistic assessments of their own performance in forming their expectations; that is, poorly performing children should hold low expectations and vice versa. At midyear the actual distributions of expectations within mark levels indicate that children are not incorporating their actual capabilities in developing their expectations but, rather, are forming their expectations independently of performance. At year-end children's expectations also continue to be formed largely independent of marks. The year-end independence is much more surprising, of course, than the independence at the time of the first report card earlier in the year, because by then two report cards have been issued. Some slight shifts have begun to appear in reading, but these shifts are small.

One can also ask whether children with high expectations are superior (or inferior) at providing accurate forecasts. Analysis indicates that, in all three substantive areas, children of all expectation levels show no significant ability to forecast their marks. All are equally unsophisticated in this respect. To sum up: using expectations alone or marks alone as predictors does not assist us in locating children who are more accurate in forecasting their first or later marks.

We now turn to a consideration of how the expectation-mark discrepance is related to change over the first-grade year and ask, for example, whether the child who did worse than he expected at first report card improves his marks. The following discussion concerns changes in both marks and expectations over first grade as a function of the expectation-mark discrepance at midyear. As a prelude to this section we must emphasize that the *discrepance* between marks and expectations is used because it incorporates more information than is contained in either marks or expectations alone and uncovers outcomes not visible when either of the other predictors is used alone.

The upper half of table 3.5 illustrates this. It is a collapsed version of a 7×7 table that related all possible types of mark changes to all possible types of reading mark-expectation discrepances at midyear. About 23% of the marks in reading went up between the middle and end of first grade, 58% remained stable, and 19% declined. If a child's year-end mark improved over his midyear mark ($N = 38$), in 63% of the cases his mark at the middle of the year had been *less* than he expected. If a child's mark declined ($N = 31$), in 39% of cases his midyear mark was *better* than he had expected. A χ^2 test on the four corners of the upper half of table 3.5 shows the association between discrepances and later improvement (or declines) in marks to be highly significant ($\chi_1^2 = 9.18$, $p < .01$). Given an initial discrepance between marks and expectations, there is a significant tendency for marks to move toward consistency with earlier expectations. Changes in performance become intelligible when previous performance is assessed in relation to previous expectations.

A more inclusive comparison, one that has an explicit causal frame of reference, can be applied to the entire table. In terms of causation, expectations higher than the marks received should lead marks to rise, expectations the same as marks should lead to no change in marks, and expectations lower than the marks received should lead marks to fall. With the margins as given, the expected values are those shown in table 3.5 in the "predicted" columns. The statistic that was used earlier to assess persistence of marks and expectations by testing for an overabundance of cases on a table diagonal can be used to test the effects of movements toward consistency just described. Such movement would lead to an excess of cases on the minor diagonal. The movement toward consistency is highly significant ($z = 2.43$, $p < .01$).

The absolute magnitude of this effect is harder to reckon because it is not equally strong for each of the types of mark change. Overall, an excess of modest proportions is involved (8.5%, or 14 of 165 cases).

Table 3.5

Changes in Reading over First Grade
as a Function of the Expectation-Mark Discrepance at Midyear

(Predicted and Observed Frequencies)

Changes in Reading Marks, T1 to T2

		Up		Same		Down		
		Pred.	Obs.	Pred.	Obs.	Pred.	Obs.	Total
Child Previously	Better	11	4	28	32	9	12	48
Did _B,S,W_ Than	Same	12	10	30	32	10	9	51
He Expected (T1)	Worse	15	24	38	32	12	10	66
	Total		38		96		31	165

Changes in Reading Expectations, T1 to T2

		Up		Same		Down		
		Pred.	Obs.	Pred.	Obs.	Pred.	Obs.	Total
Child Previously	Better	14	38	23	9	10	0	47
Did _B,S,W_ Than	Same	16	12	26	35	12	7	54
He Expected (T1)	Worse	20	0	31	36	14	29	65
	Total		50		80		36	166

As just shown, marks at the end of the school year are significantly affected by a prior mark-expectation discrepance, but there is an even stronger tendency for marks to stay the same no matter what the discrepance. Expectations, on the other hand, are more responsive to an initial discrepance, which is hardly surprising since a child's expectations are something he himself controls whereas his marks are determined by someone else and are, therefore, further removed from his direct control.

As indicated in the lower part of table 3.5, if a child received a mark higher than he expected in reading at the end of the first semester, his likely response is to increase his expectations at the end of the second semester. If he got exactly what he expected at the end of the first semester he will be rather likely to keep that expectation (but if he does change, he is about twice as likely to increase his hopes as to decrease them). If he got a lower mark than he hoped he will not increase his expectations at the end of the second semester, but he is somewhat more likely to hold to his original expectation than to lower his sights. The degree of above-chance main diagonal matching is highly significant ($z = 8.05$, $p < .01$) and amounts to almost twice what would be expected (61% compared to 33%). An important finding concerns children's receptivity to good news and their relative resistance to bad news. Given an equal discrepance, expectations are more likely to rise than to fall. We have termed this a "buoyancy effect." Expectations are more labile in a positive direction. Similar analyses of data for arithmetic and conduct (see tables 3.6 and 3.7) lead to similar outcomes. This allows us to give an overall summary of feedback effects, first for marks and then for expectations.

Whatever children get as a first mark is the "best bet" as their year-end mark, regardless of the area. There is great inertia in marks. There is also, however, a consistent (and highly significant in the case of reading and conduct, though borderline for arithmetic ($p < .10$)) movement of marks to increase consistency between marks and expectations. This tendency is not strong, involving an excess of about 8% of the cases for both reading and conduct and 4% for arithmetic, but it does occur consistently in all three of the possible ways: (1) a child's mark goes up at year-end after the child did worse than he expected at midyear, (2) a child's mark remains the same at year-end after the child got the same mark he expected at midyear, and (3) a child's mark goes down at year-end after the child did better than he expected at midyear.

Two conclusions about change in marks over the first-grade year stand out. The first is that the mark a child initially receives may have enormous importance because he will tend to get the same mark again. While persistence of a mark may be a warranted and therefore justified kind of feedback, it may also be unwarranted and provide erroneous feedback. (Later we document a lack of correspondence between marks in first grade and second grade.) The persistence of the first mark is worrisome both because this effect is strong enough to suggest a lack of mobility starting at the earliest possible point in school, before much is known about the child's talents or habits, and because it may be communicating consistently erroneous feedback. The second conclusion bears on psychological consistency, a kind of phenomenon repeatedly documented in areas of social science as far apart as dissonance theory and Freudian psychodynamics. The pattern in these data points to the discrepance between a child's expectation and his mark as a causal force acting upon children's marks over the first-grade year.

Table 3.6

Changes in Arithmetic over First Grade
as a Function of the Expectation-Mark Discrepance at Midyear

(Predicted and Observed Frequencies)

Changes in Arithmetic Marks, T1 to T2

		Up		Same		Down		
		Pred.	Obs.	Pred.	Obs.	Pred.	Obs.	Total
Child Previously	Better	11	6	29	32	2	4	42
Did B,S,W Than	Same	16	16	40	41	3	2	59
He Expected (T1)	Worse	18	23	43	39	3	2	64
	Total		45		112		8	165

Changes in Arithmetic Expectations, T1 to T2

		Up		Same		Down		
		Pred.	Obs.	Pred.	Obs.	Pred.	Obs.	Total
Child Previously	Better	11	30	21	11	10	1	42
Did B,S,W Than	Same	16	13	29	35	14	11	59
He Expected (T1)	Worse	18	2	32	36	15	27	65
	Total		45		82		39	166

Conclusions about expectations duplicate those for marks, but effects are much stronger. In all three areas (reading, arithmetic, and conduct) there is a significant tendency for children's expectations to move toward being consistent with the mark they received at midyear.

The discrepance reduction repeatedly observed here for both marks and expectations affords evidence for the construct validity of expectations as measured in this study on the one hand, and for the causal relevance of expectations for performance on the other.

The way in which discrepance reduction occurs can be specified more precisely. First, when a child gets less than he had hoped at midyear he does not lower his sights—expectations remain the same and marks tend to be brought in line. Second, if a child got more than he had hoped, his expectations immediately rise and his mark stays the same (the buoyancy effect). If the child does better than he had expected, his hopes rise; if he did worse than he expected, his marks rise.

Over the course of the first year children do get substantially better at anticipating their marks in reading (55% vs. 31% guess correctly), but the improvement is not as great for arithmetic and conduct (see table 3.8). The difference seems to arise because in reading children get better at both not underestimating and not overestimating, while for the arithmetic only overestimating declines and for conduct only underestimating declines.

Table 3.7

Changes in Conduct over First Grade
as a Function of the Expectation-Mark Discrepance at Midyear

(Predicted and Observed Frequencies)

Changes in Conduct Marks, T1 to T2

		Up		Same		Down		
		Pred.	Obs.	Pred.	Obs.	Pred.	Obs.	Total
Child Previously	Better	12	7	36	39	6	8	54
Did B,S,W Than	Same	12	8	37	40	6	7	55
He Expected (T1)	Worse	12	21	38	32	6	3	56
	Total		36		111		18	165

Changes in Conduct Expectations, T1 to T2

		Up		Same		Down		
		Pred.	Obs.	Pred.	Obs.	Pred.	Obs.	Total
Child Previously	Better	21	47	21	5	11	1	53
Did B,S,W Than	Same	23	15	23	33	12	10	58
He Expected (T1)	Worse	22	3	22	28	12	24	55
	Total		65		66		35	166

Table 3.8

Summary of Mark-Expectation Discrepances, Midyear vs. Year-End

(Percentages, N = 161)

Child Expected to Do B,S,W Than He Did, Midyear

	Reading				Arithmetic				Conduct			
	Better	Same	Worse	Total	Better	Same	Worse	Total	Better	Same	Worse	Total
Child Expected to Do B,S,W Than He Did, Year-End												
Better	18.6	5.0	8.1	31.7	14.3	5.0	6.2	25.5	16.1	11.2	8.7	36.0
Same	18.6	22.4	13.7	54.7	18.0	21.1	8.7	47.8	13.7	14.3	15.5	43.5
Worse	3.1	3.7	6.8	13.7	6.8	9.9	9.9	26.7	4.3	7.5	8.7	20.5
Total	40.4	31.1	28.6	100.0	39.1	36.0	24.8	100.0	34.2	32.9	32.9	100.0

Parents' Expectations

Before first report cards were issued in the fall parents were asked what marks they expected their children to receive in reading, arithmetic, and conduct. We found that parents were optimistic but guarded (table 3.1). The expectations of parents and children at the time of the first report card coincided only at chance levels; the percentages matching were 28.8% in reading, 37.9% in arithmetic, and 29.1% in conduct (table 3.9). At the beginning of the child's school career there is little correspondence between what parents and their children expect.

There was, nevertheless, a highly significant ($p < .01$) amount of matching between parents' expectations and marks in all three areas at the time of the first report card (table 3.10). Matching for reading declined from 55% at midyear to 49% at year-end—just enough to cause lack of a significant match at year-end. At the end of first grade, arithmetic marks still agreed significantly with parents' earlier expectations ($z = 2.67$, $p < .01$), while conduct marks at the end of first grade actually agreed better with parents' initial expectations than at midyear (56% vs. 54% agreement earlier).

What can be said about specific cases where parents' expectations and children's marks differ? Given the lack of variance in marks, it is hard for effects to display themselves; nevertheless, an interesting trend emerges. In all three areas, at both midyear and year-end, when parents were wrong they tended to err on the conservative side and to expect lower marks than their children received. The respective percentages of conservative vs. optimistic errors for reading, arithmetic, and conduct at midyear are 28% vs. 17%, 23% vs. 20%, and 27% vs. 19%; and, for year-end, 33% vs. 20%, 34% vs. 12%, and 27% vs. 17%. Only the larger differences here attain significance by themselves (e.g. arithmetic, year-end, $\chi_1^2 = 14.84$, $p < .01$), but the consistency in the direction of the differences is impressive. Parents seem to be "playing it safe," perhaps avoiding disappointment on their own part or avoiding pressuring their children by holding expectations above the child's capabilities.

How are parents able to forecast their children's first-grade marks? We have already said that we suspect parents are rather good judges of their children's IQ's (substantial correlations exist between children's IQ-test scores and parents' expectations). But this cannot be the complete story, because the correlations between IQ and marks were relatively small. To take additional factors into account in examining this question, we tabulated the child's mark against the discrepance between the child's mark and the parents' expectations. This style of analysis provides several useful kinds of information.

Table 3.9

Joint Distribution of Parents' and Children's Expectations at Midyear
Middle-Class School, Cohorts S-1 and S-2 Combined
(Percentages, N = 153 for Reading and Arithmetic, 148 for Conduct)

Children's Expectations

		Reading					Arithmetic					Conduct				
		1	2	3	4	Total	1	2	3	4	Total	1	2	3	4	Total
Parent's Expectation	1	11.1	9.8	2.6	1.3	24.8	15.0	7.8	1.3	0.6	24.8	9.5	6.8	4.7	0.7	21.6
	2	37.3	15.7	7.8	3.3	64.1	26.1	19.6	10.5	2.6	58.8	28.4	17.6	12.2	6.1	64.2
	3	7.2	--	1.3	1.3	9.8	5.2	7.8	2.0	--	15.0	6.8	2.7	2.0	1.4	12.8
	4	--	--	0.6	0.6	1.3	--	--	--	1.3	1.3	0.7	--	0.7	--	1.4
Total		55.6	25.5	12.4	6.5	100.0	46.4	35.3	13.7	4.6	100.0	45.3	27.0	20.6	8.1	100.0

Table 3.10

Joint Distribution of Middle-Class Parents' Expectations and Marks
First Report Card

(Percentages, N = 154 for Reading and Arithmetic; N = 149 for Conduct)

Marks, Time 1

	Reading				Arithmetic				Conduct				
	1	2	3	Total	1	2	3	Total	1	2	3	4	Total
Parent's Expectation, Time 1 — 1	12.3	11.0	0.6	24.0	9.1	14.9	1.3	25.3	11.4	8.7	1.3	0.0	21.5
2	20.1	39.0	5.2	64.3	11.0	43.5	3.9	58.4	19.5	36.9	8.7	0.0	65.1
3	1.3	5.2	3.9	10.4	1.9	9.1	3.9	14.9	1.3	4.7	5.4	0.7	12.1
4	0.0	1.3	0.0	1.3	0.0	0.0	1.3	1.3	0.0	0.7	0.7	0.0	1.3
Total	33.8	56.5	9.7	100.0	22.1	67.5	10.4	100.0	32.2	51.0	16.1	0.7	100.0

First, regardless of the level of their child's performance, the parents do a little better at predicting the exact mark their child will receive than would be expected by chance, but only for children displaying better-than-average performance are excesses large enough to be significant. (In absolute terms parents were most accurate for children who performed worse-than-average, but results did not attain statistical significance because small sample sizes attenuated the power of the test.)

Second, it seems parents are aware of the social norm that most children are assigned an average mark. Parents of high-ability children are the best at predicting (in the sense of significantly exceeding chance by the greatest amount, 13%, 16%, and 13% for reading, arithmetic, and conduct, respectively), but they are correct in only 37%, 41%, and 35% of the cases. This contrasts with correct predictions in 69%, 64%, and 72% of the cases for the parents of moderate-ability children, who exceed chance by only 4%, 5%, and 7%, respectively.

A third question is whether the level of parental expectations itself influences the accuracy of their expectations. An analysis similar to that reported above indicates that parents holding all levels of expectations show slightly, but not significantly, better-than-chance accuracy in forecasting, and that the largest increments above chance levels of matching do appear for those parents who hold extreme expectations.

To sum up, parents are accurate forecasters mainly because they know the "target distribution" of marks and only secondarily because they shade their opinion according to the individual child. Children at first do not seem to know the "target distribution," but they gradually become aware of it.

Parents' Expectations and Marks

Changes in marks over first grade as a function of the discrepance between parents' expectations and first marks are summarized in table 3.11 (entries on the minor diagonal again measure the extent to which children's marks move in a direction consistent with expectations). The movement is highly significant in all three performance areas.

The four corners of each of the subtables show that movement in marks is consistent with parents' expectations in both directions—marks move down as well as up to increase consistency. Inconsistent movement is rare. The overrepresentation on the minor diagonal is in line with a causal hypothesis viewing the discrepance between parents' expectations and marks at midyear as a causal variable influencing changes in children's marks between the middle of the year and the end of the year.

How does movement in marks consistent with parents' expectations

Table 3.11

Changes in Children's First-Grade Marks
as a Function of the Discrepancy between First Marks Received
and Parents' Expectations

(Predicted and Observed Scores)

Change in Reading Marks, T1 to T2

		Up		Same		Down		Total
		Pred.	Obs.	Pred.	Obs.	Pred.	Obs.	
Child Previously	Better	9	1	25	28	7	12	41
Did B,S,W Than	Same	18	18	49	50	14	13	81
Parent Expected	Worse	5	13	15	11	4	1	25
	Total		32		89		26	147

Change in Arithmetic Marks, T1 to T2

		Up		Same		Down		Total
		Pred.	Obs.	Pred.	Obs.	Pred.	Obs.	
Child Previously	Better	8	2	24	26	2	6	34
Did B,S,W Than	Same	20	19	59	63	5	2	84
Parent Expected	Worse	7	14	20	14	2	1	29
	Total		35		103		9	147

Change in Conduct Marks, T1 to T2

		Up		Same		Down		Total
		Pred.	Obs.	Pred.	Obs.	Pred.	Obs.	
Child Previously	Better	7	1	24	24	5	11	36
Did B,S,W Than	Same	15	12	52	58	10	7	77
Parent Expected	Worse	6	15	19	13	4	1	29
	Total		28		95		19	142

compare with the similar movement consistent with children's expectations? For children, the four corner cells of table 3.5 (for reading) accounted for 50 cases, of which approximately two-thirds (36) moved to
increase agreement. For parents, in the portion of table 3.11 that deals with
reading, the four corresponding corner cells account for only 27 cases, but
of these, 93% moved consistently.

In table 3.6 the movement of marks in arithmetic toward consistency
with children's expectations was not strong enough to attain significance,
whereas the movement toward consistency with parents' expectations
shown in table 3.11 is highly significant. In neither case, however, is the
movement large by practical standards for the "excess" matching accounts
for about 10% of the cases in table 3.11.

The similar table for conduct based on children's expectations for
themselves (table 3.7) likewise suggests that pressure to make performance
coincide with parents' expectations seems stronger than pressure generated
by children's expectations.

Parents' Expectations and Changes in Children's Expectations

Changes in children's expectations, unlike changes in their marks,
appear unrelated to the midyear discrepance between marks and parents'
expectations. If a child did better than his parent expected there is a slight
tendency in all three areas for the child's expectations to improve. In no
case is this association strong enough to attain significance.

This seemingly counterintuitive observation may have this basis:
When children do better than their parents expect, a large proportion of
them probably have also done better than they themselves expected. If a
child performed better than he expected, as seen earlier, there was a strong
tendency for his expectations to rise. This is what probably happened to the
children being discussed here. The cause of the expectation rise can then be
seen as positive mark feedback for the child, not the "relatively lower"
parental expectation.

Sex Differences

The most noticeable sex difference is the widening gap over the year
between the number of boys and girls given low marks in reading and
conduct. More boys than girls get the poorest mark (C) in both reading and
conduct in the middle of first grade. The odds are roughly 2:1 in both areas

Table 3.12

Distribution by Sex of Students Receiving Marks of C or Less

	Reading		Arithmetic		Conduct	
	Midyear	Year End	Midyear	Year End	Midyear	Year End
Boys	14	17	11	8	20	23
Girls	6	4	11	7	11	4
Total	20	21	22	15	31	27

that a boy rather than a girl will get a low mark. In arithmetic low marks are about equally distributed between the two sexes at midyear and year-end.

By the end of first grade teachers are even more likely to give boys the poorest marks in reading and conduct (see table 3.12), and the sex difference is highly significant.

Correlations between IQ scores and marks are given separately by sex in table 3.13, where, for the reader's convenience, combined data for the two sexes are repeated also. Differences by sex for reading and arithmetic are mixed and no patterns emerge. Differences by sex for conduct, in contrast, are striking. Whereas the correlations between IQ and conduct marks are close to zero in both cohorts at every time when data for the two sexes are aggregated, for boys alone the correlations are consistently positive, small, and not significant. For girls alone the correlations are consistently negative, larger, and significant, both for cohort S-1 and the combined cohorts. These correlations are consistent with sex-role norms. The brighter girls get better marks in conduct, whereas the conduct mark is unrelated or inversely related to IQ for boys.

Do boys and girls have different expectations for themselves when they start school? Sex-related differences in children's expectations are rather small, and what differences there are conform with sex-role norms. When expectations of children are sampled for the first time it is found that females are a little more cautious than males in both reading and arithmetic.

If parents have low expectations, are they more likely to be parents of boys or of girls? Nineteen parents expect their children to do poorly (to get a C or D) in reading, and, of these, 68% are parents of sons. The difference is not significant with a sample this size, but is in line with the well-known liability of first-grade boys to have reading problems. Of those parents (27) who expect their children to do poorly in arithmetic, a majority (56%) expect it of girls. In conduct, 21 parents expect their children to do poorly,

Table 3.13

Correlations between IQ and Marks by Sex
Middle-Class School, First Grade

	Cohort S-1			Cohort S-2			Combined Cohorts		
	N	Mean	S.D.	N	Mean	S.D.	N	Mean	S.D.
Both Sexes, IQ	91	115.4	10.1	92	111.6	11.6	183	113.5	11.0
Boys, IQ	49	115.2	10.4	51	112.4	12.5	100	113.8	11.6
Girls, IQ .	42	115.7	9.9	41	110.6	10.3	83	113.2	10.4

Correlations with IQ

	N	r	N	r	N	r
Both Sexes' Marks--Midyear						
Reading	82	-0.224*	89	-0.045	171	-0.123
Arithmetic	82	-0.022	89	-0.298**	171	-0.219**
Conduct	82	-0.109	89	-0.038	171	-0.055
Both Sexes' Marks--Year-End						
Reading	82	-0.099	90	-0.347**	172	-0.221**
Arithmetic	82	-0.008	90	-0.479**	172	-0.293**
Conduct	82	-0.043	90	-0.060	172	-0.030
Boys' Marks--Midyear						
Reading	44	-0.222	48	-0.005	92	-0.101
Arithmetic	44	0.096	48	-0.322	92	-0.183
Conduct	44	0.051	48	0.252	92	0.163
Boys' Marks--Year-End						
Reading	46	-0.196	49	-0.400**	95	-0.269**
Arithmetic	46	0.048	49	-0.507**	95	-0.253*
Conduct	46	0.093	49	0.049	95	0.104
Girls' Marks--Midyear						
Reading	38	-0.224	41	-0.102	79	-0.161
Arithmetic	38	-0.158	41	-0.260	79	-0.266*
Conduct	38	-0.341*	41	-0.252	79	-0.356**
Girls' Marks--Year-End						
Reading	36	0.037	41	-0.285	77	-0.181
Arithmetic	36	-0.131	41	-0.441**	77	-0.353**
Conduct	36	-0.337*	41	-0.271	77	-0.313**

* = significant at the .05 level.
** = significant at the .01 level.

and 71% of them expect it of a son. In sum, although parents' expectations are in the culturally predicted directions, trends here are in no case strong enough to be statistically significant.

Are boys or girls more likely to conform to low parental expectations? The majority of neither boys nor girls conform in either their marks or their expectations to low parental expectations. What is most noticeable in these cohorts is the variability of both boys' and girls' marks and expectations in the face of low parental hopes.

The picture can be viewed from another perspective. For children with low expectations, what are their parents' expectations? Parents are not likely to agree with children's low expectations. A parent having low hopes is more predictive than a child having low hopes, but both are more often wrong than right. This general pattern persists for reading, arithmetic, and conduct for both sexes, combined and individually. For example, of the boys who expect to do poorly in reading, relatively few (three out of eighteen) actually do poorly, but five have parents who expect them to do poorly. What is most impressive is that a large majority of children whose parents expect them to do poorly, or who expect to do poorly themselves, actually do well—83% of children who have low hopes get A's and B's, while 67% of children whose parents have low hopes get A's and B's.

Within-Classroom Ratings by Peers

Peer ratings within classrooms were obtained once during the school year, usually in April or May, as described in chapter 2. These ratings are probably a compound of popularity-with-peers and peers' consensus on the child's reading ability. (Small numerical values correspond to high standing and large values correspond to low standing.)

Relationships between peer rating and marks are significant and positive for both reading and arithmetic in cohort S-2 at the end of first grade, as well as for the cohorts combined (table 3.14). The correlations of peer ratings with marks increased between the end of the first semester and the end of the second semester in every instance out of nine possibilities. This is to be expected because children's choices were partially based, no doubt, on their perceptions of the teacher's evaluation of other children. The choosing for teams occurred close to the time the year-end mark was issued, and, as would be expected, the accuracy of children's perceptions sharpened over the course of the year. The relatively small size of even the year-end correlations with marks, however, suggests that peer ratings were not entirely based on academic capabilities. Sociability or popularity probably had some substantial influence, too. Peer ratings did not correlate

Table 3.14

Correlations between Peer Rating and Other Measures
Middle-Class School, First Grade

	Cohort S-1		Cohort S-2		Combined Cohorts	
	Mean = 0.503		Mean = 0.485		Mean = 0.493	
	S.D. = 0.287		S.D. = 0.304		S.D. = 0.295	
	$\underline{N}$	$\underline{r}$	$\underline{N}$	$\underline{r}$	$\underline{N}$	$\underline{r}$
IQ	73	-0.084	83	-0.347	156	-0.233**
Parent's Expectation--Midyear						
Reading	67	0.316**	69	0.318**	136	0.314**
Arithmetic	67	0.315**	69	0.225	136	0.257**
Conduct	63	0.303*	68	0.177	131	0.222*
Child's Expectation--Midyear						
Reading	71	-0.151	84	0.019	155	-0.055
Arithmetic	71	-0.131	84	0.164	155	0.013
Conduct	71	0.013	84	-0.011	155	-0.010
Child's Expectation--Year-End						
Reading	73	0.164	86	0.136	159	0.139
Arithmetic	73	-0.156	86	0.032	159	-0.059
Conduct	73	0.026	86	0.035	159	0.023
Child's Mark--Midyear						
Reading	68	0.162	84	0.122	152	0.139
Arithmetic	68	0.067	84	0.240*	152	0.173*
Conduct	68	0.014	84	0.063	152	0.040
Child's Mark--Year-End						
Reading	69	0.192	85	0.264*	154	0.225**
Arithmetic	69	0.160	85	0.318**	154	0.252**
Conduct	69	0.088	85	0.186	154	0.139

* = significant at the .05 level.
** = significant at the .01 level.

significantly with conduct marks or with children's expectations for themselves. This latter fact eliminates peer popularity from the list of possible determinants of children's expectations.

The correlation between peer rating and IQ is not significant for cohort S-1, but is highly significant for cohort S-2. When data for the two cohorts are pooled, the correlation between IQ and sociometric ranking remains highly significant although relatively small in magnitude. Intelligence thus tends to be only modestly associated with peer ratings.

With IQ partialled out there are small but still significant ($p < .05$) correlations between peer ratings and marks in both reading and arithmetic at the end of the year (N = 148, r = 0.191 for reading, r = 0.182 for arithmetic). There are no significant correlations for first-semester marks or for expectations at either time. This pattern almost exactly duplicates what appears when IQ is not controlled, except that the correlations are slightly smaller and less significant. The significant partial correlation implies that, with ability factored out, children's popularity with peers is still influenced by teachers' evaluations. Children whose academic performance is rated more highly by the teacher are also rated more highly by their classmates. Either the children are incorporating the teacher's in-class evaluations into their own social evaluations or students and teachers are using similar performance-rating procedures. Plainly, both effects could occur together and probably do. A third possibility—teachers incorporating student evaluations—is less likely.

All the correlations between parental expectations and children's peer ratings are positive, indicating that high parental expectations correspond to high standing with peers. The generally significant correlations suggest a child's parents and his peers are both responding to some characteristic of the child. It is unlikely that parental expectations cause their child's peer standing or vice versa. What characteristic both parents and peers are responding to is not apparent. It is probably neither IQ (since cohort S-1, with the weaker IQ-sociometric rating correlation, shows the stronger parent-peer agreement) nor the child's conduct (since conduct marks are essentially unrelated to peer ratings). It may be the child's physical attractiveness.

Relations between Self-Esteem Test and Expectations

Dickstein's (1972) self-esteem test, already described in chapter 2, has two forms, one for boys and one for girls. Self-esteem and marks are not correlated for either sex, and there are no systematic relationships between the self-esteem factors of this test and any other variables in this study in first grade.

Summary

Three diagrams (figures 3.1, 3.2, and 3.3) were prepared as a first step toward developing an explanatory model. The diagrams, one each for reading, arithmetic, and conduct, offer a convenient way to summarize many of the findings in this chapter. Children's expectations and marks at

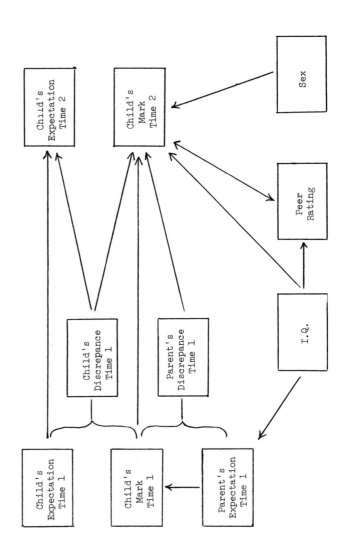

Figure 3.1
Reading Model, Middle-Class School, First Grade

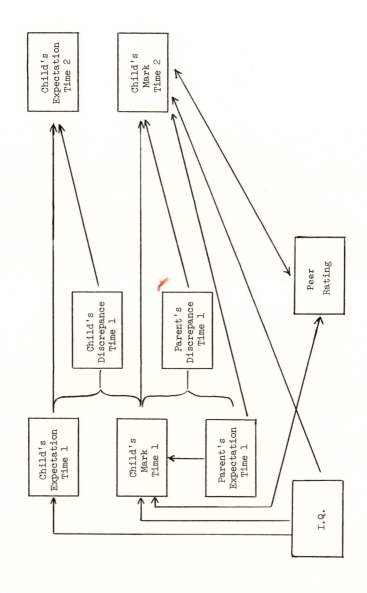

Figure 3.2

Arithmetic Model, Middle-Class School, First Grade

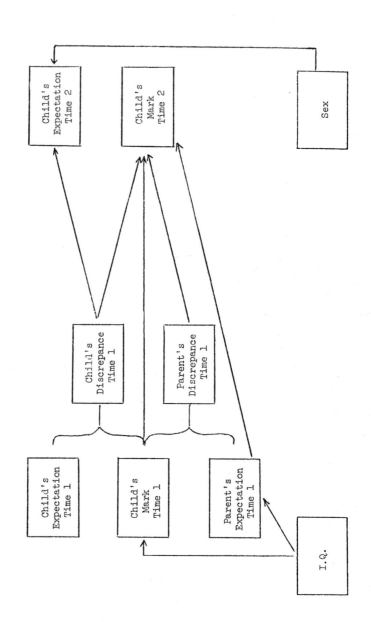

Figure 3.3
Conduct Model, Middle-Class School, First Grade

the end of first grade (T2) are taken as the outcomes of several prior variables. The diagrams are very tentative and are presented here to provide a focus for further thinking on these topics.

The arrows imply *only* an association significantly different from zero and a causal ordering in agreement with the temporal ordering. These diagrams are heuristics only; they are not path diagrams. Arrows indicate merely a relationship between two variables that was statistically significant. Figure 3.1, for example, shows that (1) midyear expectations and (2) the midyear discrepances between the children's reading expectations and their marks are significantly related to children's year-end reading expectations. Year-end reading expectations were not related to sex, IQ, sociometric rating, parents' expectations, or even directly to previous marks, so no arrows are drawn between year-end expectations and any of these variables. Year-end matching between marks and expectations is not diagrammed, since this is conceptualized as the result of the action of the other relations in the figures.

These separate figures for each area could, in the future, be combined into an overall model that would also include connections between the separate figures. It would then be possible to represent the observed consistency of marks in the different areas and other inter-area effects (for example, getting a high mark in arithmetic could influence subsequent expectations in reading). The overall model would contain several dependent variables with correlations between them, and, no doubt, correlations between the disturbance terms associated with them.

Discrepances—the gap between marks and expectations at any given time—are important predictors in first grade. They are also important conceptually, for they could imply that feedback, or reinforcement, is defined relatively, in terms of expectation levels. It is plain in all three models that the discrepance between children's midyear expectations and marks influences the children's year-end expectations, although the midyear mark itself does not. In reading and conduct this same discrepance also influences year-end marks. In all three models the discrepance between parents' expectations and children's first marks also acts upon year-end marks, and parent's expectations are causally related to initial marks in all three areas.

In comparing the model for reading with that for arithmetic, the most obvious difference is the linking of IQ with both the child's arithmetic mark and his arithmetic expectation. Sex, an element in the reading model, is not seen in the arithmetic model.

The conduct model looks different from the models for the two substantive areas. IQ has no direct effect on year-end marks or expectations,

and peer rating is not even present. There are relatively few connections in
this diagram.

In general, these first-grade children do not have initial expectations
that correspond with performance. There is clear movement toward consistency between marks and expectations over the first-grade year, however.
Feedback produces a significant movement of both marks and expectations
over the year to narrow the gap between them.

CHAPTER 4

Middle-Class Children in Second Grade

This chapter presents a brief overview of the only cohort (S-1) for which complete second-grade data are now available. By following up some of the trends that emerged in chapter 3 we are able to buttress some findings, but must discard others.

All second graders at the middle-class school in 1972–73 were studied, whether or not they had attended first grade in the same school. For analyses concerning only second-grade performance, the entire set of second graders (N = 103) was used. For assessments of changes from first grade to second grade, only data for second graders who had attended first grade in the same school (N = 80) are used.

Children's expectations declined slightly between the end of first grade and the middle of second (see tables 3.1 and 4.1), and then increased slightly over the rest of second grade. As was true for first graders, second-grade children's expectations were consistently highest in reading but differed little by subject area.

Parents of 75% of the second graders had their expectations recorded near the end of October. As was true in our study of first graders, second graders' parents' expectations were somewhat lower than their children's in all areas. From one year to the next, parents' expectations increased a little for reading (1.96 to 1.87), but decreased for arithmetic (1.83 to 2.03).

The average IQ (104.1) for this group of children turned out to be considerably lower in second grade than in first grade. (The Primary Mental Ability [PMA] test was used in first grade and the Short Form Test of Academic Aptitude [SFTAA], taken from the California Test of Mental Maturity, was used in second grade.) Both sampling variability and the fact that different IQ tests were used in the two grades could explain the difference. The correlation between the two sets of IQ scores is 0.655.

Correlations between IQ and the other measures (given in table 4.2) contrast with those seen in first grade, where significant correlations between IQ and children's expectations were entirely lacking. At the middle of second grade there are statistically significant but small correlations between IQ and both arithmetic and conduct expectations. These relationships, however, disappear by the end of second grade. Here, as was true when these children were in first grade, there are highly significant and

Table 4.1

Means, Standard Deviations for Second Grade
Cohort S-1, Middle-Class School

	N	Mean	S.D.
SFTAA I.Q.	102	104.1	11.47

Parent's Expectation--Midyear (T3)

	N	Mean	S.D.
Reading	76	1.87	0.72
Arithmetic	75	2.03	0.77
Conduct	76	1.90	0.69

Child's Expectation--Midyear (T3)

	N	Mean	S.D.
Reading	102	1.69	0.70
Arithmetic	102	1.77	0.90
Conduct	102	1.80	0.83

Child's Expectation--Year-End (T4)

	N	Mean	S.D.
Reading	102	1.63	0.63
Arithmetic	102	1.72	0.72
Conduct	102	1.68	0.63

Child's Mark--Midyear (T3)

	N	Mean	S.D.
Reading	102	1.91	0.80
Arithmetic	103	2.07	0.62
Conduct	103	1.81	0.72

Child's Mark--Year-End (T4)

	N	Mean	S.D.
Reading	103	1.60	0.65
Arithmetic	103	1.94	0.64
Conduct	103	1.73	0.73

Mark Change (Midyear Mark minus Year-End Mark, T3 - T4)

	N	Mean	S.D.
Reading	102	0.30	0.58
Arithmetic	103	0.13	0.54
Conduct	103	0.08	0.64

Child's Expectation Change
(Midyear Expectation minus Year-End Expectation, T3 - T4)

	N	Mean	S.D.
Reading	94	0.11	0.86
Arithmetic	94	0.05	1.02
Conduct	94	0.12	0.97

Child's Mark-Expectation Discrepance--Midyear (Mark minus Expectation, T3)

	N	Mean	S.D.
Reading	96	0.18	1.09
Arithmetic	97	0.31	0.96
Conduct	97	-0.01	0.88

Child's Mark-Expectation Discrepance--Year-End (Mark minus Expectation, T4)

	N	Mean	S.D.
Reading	99	-0.04	0.65
Arithmetic	99	0.21	0.67
Conduct	99	0.05	0.81

sizeable correlations between IQ and parents' expectations in reading and arithmetic, but not in conduct.

In second grade there is a definite change in the degree of matching between marks and children's expectations. Throughout first grade matching occurred at only chance levels, but by the end of second grade significant above-chance matching between marks and expectations occurs for all three areas.

Over the two-year span children display a continual tendency toward overoptimism regarding their marks only in arithmetic. This occurs in three

Table 4.2

Correlations between IQ (SFTAA) and Other Measures
Middle-Class School, Second Grade

Cohort S-1

Mean = 104.1
S.D. = 11.5

	N	r
Parent's Expectation--Midyear Second Grade		
Reading	72	-0.336**
Arithmetic	71	-0.386**
Conduct	72	-0.003
Child's Expectation--Midyear Second Grade		
Reading	96	-0.003
Arithmetic	96	-0.250*
Conduct	96	0.227*
Child's Expectation--Year-End Second Grade		
Reading	99	0.009
Arithmetic	99	-0.028
Conduct	99	0.026
Child's Mark--Midyear Second Grade		
Reading	101	-0.197*
Arithmetic	102	-0.356**
Conduct	102	0.039
Child's Mark--Year-End Second Grade		
Reading	102	-0.131
Arithmetic	102	-0.201*
Conduct	102	0.010

* = significant at the .05 level.
** = significant at the .01 level.

of the four observation periods—the exception being the end of first grade. Changes in the mark distributions, whether due to changes in the difficulty of subject matter, changes in teachers' marking severity, or other factors, influence over- or underoptimism as much as do changes in expectations themselves, however.

Changes in Children's Marks and Expectations between First and Second Grades and over Second Grade

Two facts stand out about the level of expectations between the end of first grade and the middle of second. The first is the significant consistency that characterizes expectations in all three areas. This consistency was also noted in first grade. The second is a mixed pattern of upward and downward shifts in expectations, which contrasts with a generally upward movement in first grade.

The overall pattern in matching of expectations from one time period to another can best be seen by the summary presented in table 4.3. If consistency between expectations over a time interval is taken to indicate a causal connection between expectations at the two times (either as the earlier being a direct cause of the later or both being the result of a third factor such as ability or parental expectations), the data on consistency for both first and second grades provide a fairly clear, though not totally consistent, picture of such causal relations. The pattern of matching of expectations from one time to the next indicates a much stronger push toward consistency than toward either inconsistency or a lack of consistency, however. This finding of consistency points to the importance of early experience in setting expectation levels prior to the first report card, for, once set, expectations do tend to persist.

Expectations, however, should not be thought of as being "set once and for all." To conclude this would be to overlook two things. First, the matching of expectations from one time to the next is relatively stable at about 50%, while chance levels of matching range from 38% to 46%. These percentages imply that, if a child's expectation changes, the new expectation the child holds is about as likely to persist as the earlier expectation. Thus, while a child's first expectation in an area does tend to persist, it does not seem to persist any more than his next few expectations. Examination of individual expectation histories indicates that perhaps some children display higher-than-average persistence of expectations for reading while others display lower-than-average persistence. This pattern does not hold for either arithmetic or conduct.

Second, the absolute amount of persistence is not large enough to

Table 4.3

Summary of Percentage of Expectations Matching over Time:
Middle-Class School, Cohort S-1

	Over First Grade (N=85)	From the End of First of the Middle of Second Grade (N=78)	Over Second Grade (N=94)
Reading	60**	60*	53*
Arithmetic	47*	59**	46
Conduct	45	51*	48*

* = significant at the .05 level.

** = significant at the .01 level.

produce a rigid pattern of children's expectations over time. If the probability of maintaining the same expectation from one time period to the next is 0.5, only 12.5% of the children would be expected to hold the same expectation continuously from the middle of first grade to the end of second grade, assuming independence and nonstratification of transition probabilities—assumptions that the data suggest are reasonable. A significant persistence of expectations is present, but the degree of persistence contradicts, at least for middle-class children, the idea that a child's expectations crystallize soon after he starts school and are refractory to change thereafter.

It should also be noted that children with low expectations do not provide many cases of matched expectations. The majority of children expecting C's and D's at any one time hold expectations for average or high marks by the next time they are interviewed.

Turning now to a consideration of the stability of individual children's marks over time, we note that about two-thirds of the children received identical marks at midyear and the end of the year in each of the three areas (a highly significant matching, $p < .01$), similar to the matching of year-end and midyear marks in first grade. Both these within-grade observations are in sharp contrast to the lack of significant matching between first-grade marks and second-grade marks. The mismatch between marks at the end of first grade and the middle of second grade departs radically from the consistency shown within years.

Two explanations are possible. First, because in this school each child's performance is evaluated according to that child's own ability, any given teacher may be quite consistent in her evaluation of a child's scholastic efforts, but that evaluation may differ substantially from another teacher's evaluation of the effort. Second, there could be a child-by-year interaction such that each school year provides a steady set of environmental variables throughout the year for a child, but the set changes between years (the set consisting of teacher personalities, presence of a child's best friend in his class, and so on). If children's efforts interact with other variables—that is, if different environments stimulate or depress different children—the observed pattern of mark consistency would also be observed. In fact, a mixture of these two models probably prevails.

For the marks that do not match from one time to the next, do mark increases or declines predominate? Table 4.4 summarizes changes in marks. Conduct marks, for the most part, do not increase or decrease throughout the first two years. Arithmetic marks increase over the first year to a point where they are very high at year-end—41% get A's. The drop in arithmetic marks from the end of first grade to the middle of second grade is more than getting back to a "reasonable" mark distribution, though, for arithmetic marks at midyear of second grade are the lowest assigned in any area at any time (2.07). When arithmetic marks again rise over the second year they do not rise above their mid-first-grade level.

The rise in reading marks over the second year to the highest average observed (1.60) must create "personnel management" problems for the third-grade teacher. This teacher will be forced to mark comparatively hard to produce any variability at all among children in third grade and ex-

Table 4.4

Summary of Increases or Decreases in Marks over Time:
Middle-Class School, Cohort S-1

	T1 to T2		T2 to T3		T3 to T4	
	Increase	Decrease	Increase	Decrease	Increase	Decrease
Reading	21	14	18	27	33 **	4
Arithmetic	19 **	5	10 **	38	20 *	8
Conduct	12	13	25	20	22	14

* = significant difference between number of increases and decreases at the .05 level using χ^2_1.

** = significant difference between number of increases and decreases at the .01 level using χ^2_1.

tremely hard if children's marks are to show some improvement over the third-grade year.

Expectations in Different Areas

Matching between children's expectations in reading and arithmetic at the end of second grade (41%) is not significant and contrasts with the significant undermatching observed throughout first grade. By the end of second grade the children seem to have overcome whatever it was that made them initially expect different marks in reading and arithmetic, but they show no recognition of the continuing consistency in the teachers' assignment of reading and arithmetic marks. Only the degree of matching predicted by chance is present also between expectations in arithmetic and conduct and between those in reading and conduct. At the end of second grade few children (an average of about 1.5%) held low expectations (for C's or D's) in two areas simultaneously, and none held low expectations in all three areas.

Discrepance Effects

As before, we see that the discrepance between earlier marks and expectations leads to change. Table 4.5 presents the changes in marks that occurred between the middle of second grade and the end of second grade as a function of mark-expectation discrepances at the middle of second grade. In all three areas mark changes over the second year tend to follow the direction of the initial discrepance between marks and expectations. As in first grade, only a modest proportion of the cases is involved in the overrepresentation on the minor diagonal, 15%, 8%, and 9% for reading, arithmetic, and conduct, respectively, and the majority of these changes are an improvement in mark when expectations were higher than a previous mark. The concordance in movement toward consistency for both first and second grades is impressive, especially since, in second grade, as earlier, the relative inertia of marks prevails.

Table 4.6 shows the changes in expectations during second grade resulting from the various possible types of midyear mark-expectation discrepances for reading, arithmetic, and conduct. Again, there is movement to bring about consistency, with highly significant effects occurring in all three areas. During second grade children's expectations tended to (1) move up if they earlier had received a better mark than they expected, (2) move down if they earlier had received a mark worse than they expected, or (3) stay the same if they earlier received exactly what they expected.

Table 4.5

Joint Distribution of Expectation-Mark Discrepance at Time 3
and Change in Marks from Time 3 to Time 4, Cohort S-1

(Predicted and Observed Scores)

Reading
Mark Went U,S,D from Time 3 to Time 4

		Up		Same		Down		Total
		Pred.	Obs.	Pred.	Obs.	Pred.	Obs.	
Child Previously	Better	8	2	17	22	1	2	26
Did B,S,W Than	Same	11	8	23	26	1	1	35
He Expected (T3)	Worse	11	21	23	14	1	0	35
	Total		31		62		3	96

Arithmetic
Mark Went U,S,D from Time 3 to Time 4

		Up		Same		Down		Total
		Pred.	Obs.	Pred.	Obs.	Pred.	Obs.	
Child Previously	Better	4	3	14	15	1	1	19
Did B,S,W Than	Same	7	4	25	29	3	2	35
He Expected (T3)	Worse	9	13	31	26	3	4	43
	Total		20		70		7	97

Conduct
Mark Went U,S,D from Time 3 to Time 4

		Up		Same		Down		Total
		Pred.	Obs.	Pred.	Obs.	Pred.	Obs.	
Child Previously	Better	6	3	17	19	3	4	26
Did B,S,W Than	Same	10	7	30	32	6	7	46
He Expected (T3)	Worse	5	11	16	12	3	2	25
	Total		21		63		13	97

Table 4.6

Joint Distribution of Expectation-Mark Discrepance at Time 3
and Change in Expectations from Time 3 to Time 4, Cohort S-1

(Predicted and Observed Scores)

Reading
Expectations Went U,S,D from Time 3 to Time 4

		Up		Same		Down		Total
		Pred.	Obs.	Pred.	Obs.	Pred.	Obs.	
Child Previously	Better	7	18	14	8	5	0	26
Did B,S,W Than	Same	9	7	17	22	7	3	32
He Expected (T3)	Worse	9	0	18	18	7	16	34
	Total		25		48		19	92

Arithmetic
Expectations Went U,S,D from Time 3 to Time 4

		Up		Same		Down		Total
		Pred.	Obs.	Pred.	Obs.	Pred.	Obs.	
Child Previously	Better	5	14	8	4	5	0	18
Did B,S,W Than	Same	10	11	16	19	9	4	34
He Expected (T3)	Worse	11	1	19	20	11	20	41
	Total		26		43		24	93

Conduct
Expectations Went U,S,D from Time 3 to Time 4

		Up		Same		Down		Total
		Pred.	Obs.	Pred.	Obs.	Pred.	Obs.	
Child Previously	Better	8	19	12	7	6	0	26
Did B,S,W Than	Same	12	7	20	28	10	7	42
He Expected (T3)	Worse	7	1	12	9	6	15	25
	Total		27		44		22	93

Both marks and expectations were reasonably stable during second grade. Marks remained the same at both times 3 and 4 in 65%, 72%, and 65% of the cases for reading, arithmetic, and conduct, respectively. Expectations were more variable, yet they remained the same in 52%, 46%, and 47% of the cases for the respective areas. Despite this basic backdrop of consistency, the same causal patterns that accounted for change in first grade are clearly visible within second grade. Furthermore, causal effects of a preceding mark-expectation discrepance on both marks and expectations appear *between* first and second grades as well (table 4.7). All the diagonal cells that would indicate changes in the direction of consistency reveal overrepresentation, even when the overrepresentation does not attain significance.

The results altogether are encouraging. There are similar causal patterns within both years as well as between years in the middle-class school. As in first grade, the rise in expectations following the receipt of a better mark than expected (69%, 78%, and 73%) is more pronounced than the fall in expectations when marks were worse than expected (47%, 49%, and 69%). The buoyancy effect—marks and expectations moving up to close an initial discrepancy more readily than they move down—then, continues within second grade for reading, arithmetic, and conduct marks, but not for conduct expectations. (Conduct contrasts with the other two areas in that negative feedback produces downward expectation revision with nearly the same certainty as positive feedback produces upward revision.)

The buoyancy effect, however, does not operate between years. For changes in marks between first and second grades, downward movement following receipt of a mark that was higher than expected is, if anything, more likely than an upward movement following receipt of a lower mark than expected. For reading, arithmetic, and conduct, respectively, the percentages of marks moving down if a lower mark had been expected are 50%, 62%, and 58%, and the percentages moving up after the expectation of a higher mark are 44%, 17%, and 61%. The expectation part of the buoyancy effect has also largely disappeared between first and second grades, since expectations are about as likely to move down if a child's expectation exceeded his mark (32%, 41%, and 50%) as they are to move up if a child's mark exceeded his expectation (36%, 50%, and 45%). The buoyancy effect manifests itself within both years but is not present between years.

It should be kept in mind in assessing the data for both years that this overall style of analysis ignores regression effects. Some of the combinations of marks and expectations counted in the "better" and "worse" categories are based on extreme marks and/or expectations, and some regression from these extremes would be expected to occur by the time of subsequent observations. Although such confounding is certainly possible,

Table 4.7

Main or Minor Diagonal Matching in the Direction of Consistency
between Time 2 and Time 3, Middle-Class School

	Changes in Marks	Changes in Expectations
Reading	z = 2.78**	z = 1.05
Arithmetic	z = 1.01	z = 3.62**
Conduct	z = 4.33**	z = 2.58**

* = significant at the .05 level.

** = significant at the .01 level.

two kinds of evidence indicate regression is not the only effect present. First, buoyancy cannot be explained as a regression effect, for regression, if present, should be roughly equivalent at both extremes. The buoyancy effect is present within both first and second grades and is lopsided both for marks and expectations. Second, an initial matching of marks and expectations leads repeatedly to an overrepresentation of cases that display no change in marks or expectations. Since a regression effect can produce only a *change* in a variable over time, observing more stability than expected implicates some other causal mechanism. Thus, while regression effects may exist, they are not sufficient to account for all the findings by any means.*

The analysis may actually underrate causal effects, because changes in marks due to concurrent expectations may masquerade as evidence against the causal effect of earlier mark-expectation discrepancies. Suppose a child expects a high mark and receives a high mark at time T_0, for example. If this child now revises his expectations downward, and his mark declines by T_1, such a case would be counted as evidence contradict-

---

*We should also note that constraints on the possible combinations of marks and expectations (collinearity) in the 3×3 discrepancy-change tables produce a slight positive bias in the matching tests we used. That is, the matching tests are slightly more likely to attain significance than completely unbiased procedures would be. The same patterns of findings as those reported here and elsewhere in this book, however, are found with unbiased procedures developed since this book went to press. Small feedback effects of children's expectations on their marks continue to be the rule, with feedback parameters bordering on statistical significance.

We nevertheless believe that the analyses reported in this book *do* reflect the attribution processes used by children, parents, and teachers to "explain" the mark-expectation linkages they see. These analyses model the causal structure seen by the actors in the social system. They actually have no way to partial out the structural constraints inherent in the system, nor of estimating the strengths of the complex causal forces that can be isolated only through use of elaborate computer routines.

ing the discrepance analysis—marks and expectations would have changed following no initial discrepance. Yet the true explanation for the observed mark change clearly implicates expectations. More nearly continuous measurement of children's expectations would be required to investigate such possibilities, but in this study such effects produce bias against, rather than for, the causal efficacy of expectations.

Parents' Expectations

In our study of second graders 71% of the parents who had given their expectations when their children were in first grade did so again. Most parents continued to "play it safe" by expecting a mark of B. Parents tended to hold the same expectation in first and second grades to a highly significant degree for arithmetic and conduct (63%, $z = 3.30$, 67%, $z = 3.68$, respectively), but not for reading (53%). In all three areas, however, parents' second-grade expectations strongly and significantly matched the marks their children received at the end of first grade (61%, 54%, and 66%). This matching may stem from a spurious relationship, with parents' first-grade expectation as the independent variable. Parents' first-grade arithmetic and conduct expectations matched their second-grade expectations, so if their first expectations also matched children's marks at the end of the first year (as was true for arithmetic and conduct) the observed matching between second-grade expectations and first-grade marks may have reflected the fact that both variables agreed with parents' time 1 expectations. None of even the significant relationships is particularly strong, however, so it seems more likely (especially for reading) that parents are bringing their expectations into line with their child's performance.

The discrepance between parents' expectations and their children's marks can be considered a causal (independent) variable, just as a similar discrepance for children was earlier examined for its causal effect. The two entities that might change in response to such a discrepance are the child's marks and the parents' expectations.

First, the causal efficacy of a discrepance between parental expectations and first marks (at mid-first grade) on parental expectations is clear. In all three areas parental expectations change from mid-first grade to mid-second grade so as to significantly increase the consistency between marks and expectations ($p < .01$). The overrepresentation of cases on the main diagonals in table 4.8 ($z = 4.59$, $z = 4.03$, and $z = 4.23$ for reading, arithmetic, and conduct, respectively) indicates that parents modified their expectations upward if the child did better than expected, maintained the

Table 4.8

Distribution of Parental Expectation-Mark Discrepance at Time 1
and Changes in Parental Expectations from Time 1 to Time 3, Cohort S-1
(Predicted and Observed Scores)

Reading

Parental Expectation Went U,S,D from T1 to T3

		Up		Same		Down		Total
		Pred.	Obs.	Pred.	Obs.	Pred.	Obs.	
Child Did B,S,W	Better	5	14	8	2	2	0	16
Than Parent	Same	12	4	19	25	5	7	36
Expected at T1	Worse	2	1	4	4	1	2	7
	Total		19		31		9	59

Arithmetic

Parental Expectation Went U,S,D from T1 to T3

		Up		Same		Down		Total
		Pred.	Obs.	Pred.	Obs.	Pred.	Obs.	
Child Did B,S,W	Better	2	6	6	4	2	0	10
Than Parent	Same	6	4	23	27	7	5	36
Expected at T1	Worse	2	0	8	6	3	7	13
	Total		10		37		12	59

Conduct

Parental Expectation Went U,S,D from T1 to T3

		Up		Same		Down		Total
		Pred.	Obs.	Pred.	Obs.	Pred.	Obs.	
Child Did B,S,W	Better	3	6	9	5	2	3	14
Than Parent	Same	7	4	22	29	6	2	35
Expected at T1	Worse	1	1	4	1	1	4	6
	Total		11		35		9	55

same expectation if the child did the same as expected, or revised their expectations downward if the child did worse than expected on the first report card. This is somewhat surprising given the time interval involved—parents have received two other report cards in the intervening time. Either the first report card had an unusually large impact or later report cards provided parents with the same feedback as the first. (Some recent evidence underscores the "effect of primacy" on forming expectations when conditions are carefully balanced [Feldman & Allen, 1974]. In tutoring experiments, tutees who were good at the start and whose performance later deteriorated caused tutors to hold higher expectations than tutees who were poor at the start and later improved.)

On the other hand, our data do provide support for the "similar repeated feedback" interpretation. Parents' reading expectations moved significantly toward consistency ($z = 4.84$, $p < .01$) with their children's midyear marks if their child received the same mark at midyear and year-end, while no significant ($z = 0.25$) movement was observed if their child received different (either higher or lower) reading marks at midyear and year-end. For arithmetic and conduct, equally strong movement of parental expectations toward consistency with midyear marks was observed whether marks changed or were the same at midyear and year-end.

It remains debatable, therefore, whether a "primacy" or a "repeated feedback" model is appropriate. What is unambiguously known, though, is that parents' expectations in all three areas moved significantly toward consistency with their children's first marks.

In considering the effect parents' expectations have on children's marks, we found that the second-grade year parental expectation-mark discrepancy had a significant effect on children's reading marks ($z = 3.73$, $p < .01$) during the second year (time 3 to time 4), but no significant effect for either arithmetic ($z = 1.35$) or conduct ($z = 1.00$) marks. For reading, the changes that occurred in marks subsequent to the second-grade parental expectation-mark discrepancy are all of the type where marks increase to reduce the discrepancy or stay the same following no discrepancy. In none of the 11 cases where marks exceeded parental expectations did the child's mark fall.

The same caution expressed for first-grade data holds here: when a child's mark is lower than his parent's expectation, his mark is also likely to be lower than he himself expected, since parents generally have lower expectations than their children. The child's expectation-mark discrepancy could just as well be the cause of a mark increase. Thus a mark increase may be owing to the parent's and/or the child's discrepancy. The fact that the causal efficacy of the children's discrepancy is significant in all areas while the causal efficacy of the parents' discrepancy is significant only for reading indicates that one must be more concerned with confounding effects when examining parental discrepancies (as we are here) than when examining children's discrepancies.

Overall, the impact of parents' expectations on performance is substantial in first grade—at least it is larger than the impact of children's expectations. By second grade, however, parents apparently rely more on their child's report card marks than on whatever clues they used to estimate performance before they saw his report card. The result is a "persistence forecast" by parents in second grade, a forecast that minimizes the average size of the parent's expectation-mark discrepancy when marks are consistent from one period to the next. This strategy, although it is sensible, has the consequence of diminishing the impact of parental expectations.

It is remarkable that parents' expectations do not match their children's expectations in any area at any time in second grade, replicating what was noted in first grade. At least in this cohort, therefore, children do not simply adopt their parents' expectations. For the cases where parents' and children's expectations do not match, the parent's expectation is lower than the child's expectation in reading and arithmetic (midyear $\chi_1^2 = 4.02$, $p < .05$ and $\chi_1^2 = 10.50$, $p < .01$; year-end $\chi_1^2 = 4.02$, $p < .05$ and $\chi_1^2 = 8.31$, $p < .01$ for reading and arithmetic, respectively), as an examination of the means in table 4.1 would lead one to expect.

The relationship between parents' expectations and children's marks in second grade also continues the general pattern observed in first grade. Parents' expectations match their children's marks to a significant degree in all areas throughout second grade, with the exception of year-end conduct marks. At midyear 65%, 68%, and 51% matched for reading, arithmetic, and conduct, respectively. At year-end the percentages matching were 67%, 56%, and 44% (conduct not significant).

In short, parents' expectations in second grade behaved in relation to their children's marks and expectations much as they did in first grade, showing definite relationships to children's marks and no relationship to children's expectations. The causal impact of the parental mark-expectation discrepancy on marks, however, is considerably reduced. The movement of parental expectations between first and second grades to bring them into line with first-grade marks results in a "persistence forecast" that leads to parents' expectations having little effect on second-grade marks.

Sex Differences

At the end of second grade there are relatively few marks below a B given in reading to either sex (only 7%), but girls do get more A's. In arithmetic the average mark for the two sexes is almost identical (1.91 for boys compared to 1.89 for girls). In conduct there is a strong trend for girls to get better marks. Over 60% of the girls got A's and only 8% got C's (no D's), whereas a relatively large percentage of boys got C's or D's (20%) and only 28% received A's.

Marks in reading show girls expending greater effort (or displaying greater ability) over the first two grades and receiving a disproportionate share of A's, starting from an approximately equal assignment of A's on the first report card. Arithmetic marks show very little difference in average level by sex at any time. In conduct girls outperform boys at every marking period, which is not a surprising finding. For this cohort there are stronger relations between IQ and marks in second grade than were found in first grade, but the persistence of sharp differences in these correlations for the two sexes (see table 4.9) is perhaps even more interesting. In the two substantive areas correlations are about the same for the two sexes, especially if one considers the smaller variability of girls' marks. In conduct, however, the same "suppressor effect" associated with sex seen in first grade can be seen here. For boys there is a nonsignificant positive association between IQ and conduct marks (high IQ is associated with low marks), while for girls there is a negative and significant (at midyear) association between IQ and conduct marks. The correlations by sex are consistent with cultural sex norms.

In second grade, high expectations continue to predominate for both sexes in reading and arithmetic, and the sexes still do not differ significantly in expectations in any area. By the end of second grade, for the first time, less than 50% of the boys expect an A in reading, while a majority of the girls (55%) still look for an A in reading (a smaller majority than heretofore). Likewise, there has been considerable moderation in boys' expectations for arithmetic, even though the modal category (47%) is for an A. For girls there is also a noticeable moderation, the modal category (50%) now being for a B. In conduct there are slightly fewer low expectations for both sexes at the end of second grade, and, again, the sexes remain similar. It seems, then, that the two sexes do not differ in expectations over the two-year period (conduct at time 2 is the only exception).

Self-Esteem Test in Second Grade

The same self-esteem test that had been administered in the spring of first grade was administered in the spring of second grade. No patterns

Table 4.9

Correlation between IQ (SFTAA) and Marks by Sex
Cohort S-1, Middle-Class School, Second Grade

	N	Mean	S.D.
Combined Sexes, IQ	102[†]	104.1	11.5
Boys, IQ	54	105.4	12.9
Girls, IQ	47	102.8	9.7

	Correlations with IQ	
	N	r
Combined Sexes' Marks--Midyear		
Reading	101	-0.197*
Arithmetic	102	-0.356**
Conduct	102	0.039
Combined Sexes' Marks--Year-End		
Reading	102	-0.131
Arithmetic	102	-0.201*
Conduct	102	0.010
Boys' Marks--Midyear		
Reading	54	-0.212
Arithmetic	54	-0.408*
Conduct	54	0.157
Boys' Marks--Year-End		
Reading	54	-0.196
Arithmetic	54	-0.201
Conduct	54	0.062
Girls' Marks--Midyear		
Reading	46	-0.257
Arithmetic	47	-0.304*
Conduct	47	-0.294*
Girls' Marks--Year-End		
Reading	47	-0.093
Arithmetic	47	-0.201
Conduct	47	-0.153

[†] The sex of one child was not ascertained.
* = significant at the .05 level.
** = significant at the .01 level.

Table 4.10

Correlations between Second-Grade Self-Esteem Scores and Other Measures
Middle-Class School, Cohort S-1 in Second Grade

	Boys				Girls			
		N	Mean	S.D.		N	Mean	S.D.
Factor I	"Boy Scout"	54	0.00	1.0	"Achiever"	46	-0.02	1.0
Factor II	"Athlete"	54	0.00	1.0	"Athlete"	46	0.01	1.0
Factor III	"Scholar"	54	-0.05	1.0	"Social"	46	-0.03	1.0

	Boys'				Girls'			
	N	Factor I r	Factor II r	Factor III r	N	Factor I r	Factor II r	Factor III r
Parent's Expectation--Midyear Second Grade, Time 3								
Reading	41	-0.084	-0.091	-0.134	30	0.367*	0.399*	0.367*
Arithmetic	40	-0.160	-0.146	-0.230	30	0.237	0.398*	0.250
Conduct	41	-0.564**	-0.180	-0.368*	30	0.022	0.028	0.033
Child's Expectation--Midyear Second Grade, Time 3								
Reading	49	-0.198	0.191	-0.288*	44	-0.265	-0.416**	-0.243
Arithmetic	49	-0.331*	-0.411**	-0.534**	44	-0.216	-0.118	-0.096
Conduct	49	-0.385**	-0.392**	-0.132	44	0.043	0.004	0.0
Child's Expectation--Year-End Second Grade, Time 4								
Reading	52	-0.356**	0.034	-0.308*	45	-0.254	-0.145	-0.062
Arithmetic	52	-0.317*	-0.186	-0.446**	45	-0.228	-0.217	-0.146
Conduct	52	-0.039	0.037	0.023	45	-0.232	-0.159	-0.137
Child's Mark--Midyear Second Grade, Time 3								
Reading	53	-0.113	-0.002	-0.026	44	0.168	0.317*	0.278
Arithmetic	53	0.071	-0.074	-0.043	45	-0.118	0.174	0.096
Conduct	53	-0.493**	-0.072	-0.341*	45	-0.097	0.138	0.055

Table 4.10(Continued)

	Boys' N	Factor I r	Factor II r	Factor III r	Girls' N	Factor I r	Factor II r	Factor III r
Child's Mark--Year-End Second Grade, Time 4								
Reading	53	-0.276*	-0.137	-0.285*	45	0.017	0.209	0.205
Arithmetic	53	-0.224	-0.194	-0.297*	45	-0.082	0.144	0.049
Conduct	53	-0.310*	-0.001	-0.030	45	-0.235	0.038	-0.027
Grade 1 Self-Esteem Scores								
Factor I	43	0.357*	0.169	0.265	31	-0.116	-0.001	-0.162
Factor II	43	0.436**	0.520**	0.372*	31	0.181	0.381*	0.051
Factor III	43	0.308*	0.499**	0.437**	31	-0.039	0.055	-0.081
Grade 2 Self-Esteem Scores								
Factor I	54	1.000	0.202	0.670**	46	1.000	0.556**	0.744**
Factor II	54	0.202	1.000	0.219	46	0.556**	1.000	0.516**
Factor III	54	0.670**	0.219	1.000	46	0.744**	0.516**	1.000

* = significant at the .05 level.
** = significant at the .01 level.

appeared in first grade, but they did emerge in second grade. A glance at table 4.10 reveals that the results are very different for boys and girls.

For boys there is substantial test-retest reliability on all three factor* scores, considering the 12- to 13-month time difference. The correlation between the scores on factor I (the boy scout self-image) as measured in first grade and in second grade is significant ($r = 0.357$, $p < .05$). The over-time correlation for factor II (the athlete self-image) is much more substantial and is highly significant ($r = 0.520$, $p < .01$), as is the correlation for factor III (the student or scholar self-image) ($r = 0.437$, $p < .01$).

Two sets of significant correlations for boys are intuitively understandable. First, it is reasonable that a boy's student self-image (factor III) correlate significantly with his expectations for both reading and arithmetic throughout second grade and with his year-end reading and arithmetic marks. Likewise, it is reasonable that a boy's boy scout or good citizen self-image correlate significantly with his parents' conduct expectation, his mid-second-grade conduct expectation, and his conduct marks throughout second grade. Several of the remaining significant correlations for boys may result from the correlations among the different self-esteem subsection scores. For example, the correlations between boys' second-grade academic expectations and marks and the boy scout self-image may be partly the result of the substantial correlation between boys' student self-image and athletic self-image ($r = 0.670$, $p < .01$). The pattern of correlations for midyear and year-end do not coincide very well, establishing an inconsistency that is troubling.

For girls the picture is totally different from that seen for boys during the second year. The only factor to show a significant over-time stability is athletic self-image ($r = 0.381$, $p < .05$), and this is the only factor that correlates significantly with either marks or expectations. No likely explanation exists for this finding.

For girls, all correlations of self-esteem factors with parents' second-grade expectations are positive (indicating that high self-esteem is associated with low parental expectations), in contrast to the completely negative correlations for boys. Girls with high self-esteem may be less dependent on parents, leading parents (mothers) to interact with them less and to underestimate their capabilities in reading. Complex parent effects within and across sex are often alluded to (Hennig, 1971).

---

*The use of the term "factor" here is intended to convey the fact that the subsections of the self-esteem test were originally based on a factor analysis. The self-esteem scores used for the correlations are actually within-cohort z-scores that are based on a summated rating of the items relating to each subsection of the self-esteem test. See the discussion of this measure in chapter 2.

Absences

Data for absences (the total number of days absent during a school year) were not tallied until the 1972–73 school year. Thus we have data only for cohort S-2 in first grade and cohort S-1 in second grade. The average number of absences for cohort S-2 in first grade is 8.78, with a standard deviation of 5.70. None of the cohort S-2 first-grade correlations involving absences is significant (N's range from 73 for parents' conduct expectations to over 90 for all correlations with children's marks and expectations).

For cohort S-1 in second grade the average number of absences is 7.60, with a standard deviation of 5.81. For this cohort the only correlation between absences and marks significant beyond the 5% level is that for reading marks at midyear second grade, although several other correlations approach significance—arithmetic marks at midyear and reading and conduct marks at year-end (see table 4.11). None of the correlations between children's expectations and absences is significant, but there is a highly significant correlation between parents' expectations for arithmetic and absences.

That the largest correlation involves parents' forecasts is interesting. Absenteeism is cumulative for the entire year, while parents' expectations were secured by interviews at a single time, early in the year. Do parents with low expectations keep their children home more often? The significant second-grade arithmetic correlation might indicate this, but the other parent-expectation correlations are not significant, so it seems that no clear answer may be drawn from these data.

It might be argued that the restricted range of the absence variable suppresses correlations, since, with standard deviations of 5.7 and 5.8 days, there may not be enough variability in the absence scores for significant correlations to emerge. (As we demonstrate in chapter 5, in the working-class school, where the variability of absenteeism is considerably greater, parental expectations in both substantive scholastic areas display highly significant correlations with absenteeism.) Alternatively, and perhaps more veridically, the smaller standard deviation itself may be an indication that parental expectations do not strongly influence absenteeism in the middle-class school. Since we observed the entire range of the actual absence scores available in this school, it is not reasonable to postulate the effects of hypothetically larger ranges. Rather, both the low average number of absences and the fact that they do not vary much suggest absences will not be a likely source of explanation for significant variance in results in the middle-class school.

Table 4.11

Correlations between Absences and Other Measures
Middle-Class School, Second Grade

Cohort S-1

Mean = 7.60

S.D. = 5.81

	N	r
Parent's Expectation--Midyear Second Grade		
Reading	72	0.113
Arithmetic	71	0.301**
Conduct	72	0.002
Child's Expectation--Midyear Second Grade		
Reading	97	-0.077
Arithmetic	97	0.140
Conduct	97	-0.121
Child's Expectation--Year-End Second Grade		
Reading	100	-0.022
Arithmetic	100	0.088
Conduct	100	0.144
Child's Mark--Midyear Second Grade		
Reading	102	0.277*
Arithmetic	103	0.177
Conduct	103	0.065
Child's Mark--Year-End Second Grade		
Reading	103	0.174
Arithmetic	103	0.093
Conduct	103	0.180

* = significant at the .05 level.
** = significant at the .01 level.

Standardized Achievement

The most crucial question about children's expectations and others'
expectations for them can be raised in terms of standardized performance
measures. When it comes to the real world, what counts is performance—
the ability to demonstrate competence in reading and arithmetic. Teachers'
marks have some validity for predicting competence, but they reflect many
variables besides children's sheer ability to read or to do arithmetic. For

one thing, teachers who have spent a considerable time in a particular school may develop marking "anchor points" based on their experiences in that school. A teacher in a school where children are above average in intelligence may tend to downgrade the performance of an average-IQ child more than she would if a national sample of children formed her comparison group. For another thing, teachers' marks, unlike standardized test scores, are a compound of many variables besides actual performance, including school marking policies and considerations of what mark is likely to have an optimal effect on the child's motivation at this point in his development.

It is also important to establish that there is a substantial correlation between marks and standardized achievement because marks have been invoked as a measure of performance in much of the preceding discussion. (As is demonstrated shortly, marks do correlate strongly with standardized test scores in reading and arithmetic, especially at midyear.) The most pressing reason for utilizing standardized achievement measures, however, is to allow comparisons from one school to another.

Standardized measures and some limited data related to them have, therefore, been included for cohort S-1 even though they are outside the time boundaries (first and second grades) of the remainder of the analyses presented in this book. Children in cohort S-1, who began first grade in September 1971, took no standardized achievement tests until third grade. They then took the Iowa Tests of Basic Skills. In what follows, the Iowa tests in reading, arithmetic, and work-study habits are taken as standardized tests of reading, arithmetic, and conduct, paralleling the three marking areas that have served as the focus of performance in this study until now.*

These middle-class children are doing well in terms of national norms; in the second half of third grade they performed above the beginning fourth-grade level in all areas: 4.6 in reading, 4.3 in arithmetic, and 4.4 in work-study habits.

The correlations between marks and standardized achievement scores are substantial in reading and arithmetic for first-grade marks, second-grade marks, and third-grade marks. Correlations are uniformly higher at midyear than at year-end (table 4.12). The explanation for this within-year

---

*Actually, scores on six achievement subtests were available: Mathematical Concepts, Mathematical Problems, Arithmetic Total, Vocabulary, Reading, and Work-Study Habits. Since Arithmetic Total is a combination of Mathematical Concepts and Mathematical Problems, and since both parts behaved statistically much like the total, only Arithmetic Total is used. The Work-Study Habits subtest was used as a parallel indicator of conduct even though "conduct" implies much more than work-study habits. All test scores are recorded as grade level equivalents, so 2.5, for example, would indicate performance at a level equivalent to that of an average child when he is halfway through second grade.

Table 4.12

Correlation of Standardized Achievement Test Scores (Obtained Late in Third Grade) with Other Measures, Middle-Class School, Cohort S-1

Standardized Achievement	N	Mean	S.D.	Time 1 N	Time 1 r	Time 2 N	Time 2 r	Time 3 N	Time 3 r	Time 4 N	Time 4 r	Time 5 N	Time 5 r	Time 6 N	Time 6 r
Reading	98	4.61	1.07												
Arithmetic	98	4.28	0.86												
Conduct(Work-Study)	97	4.44	0.85												
Parent's Expectation															
Reading				69	-0.296*			59	-0.673**			70	-0.693**		
Arithmetic				69	-0.271*			59	-0.376**			70	-0.510**		
Conduct				65	0.119			59	0.182			70	-0.148		
Child's Expectation															
Reading				74	-0.024	74	-0.161	77	-0.033	83	-0.341**	86	-0.358***	84	-0.451**
Arithmetic				74	-0.268*	74	-0.276*	77	-0.215	83	-0.179	86	-0.427***	84	-0.476**
Conduct				74	-0.126	74	-0.122	77	-0.001	83	-0.131	86	0.034	84	-0.023
Child's Mark															
Reading				71	-0.448**	74	-0.343**	82	-0.726**	83	-0.545**	80	-0.684***	83	-0.366**
Arithmetic				71	-0.333**	74	-0.235*	83	-0.513**	83	-0.475**	88	-0.541**	89	-0.424**
Conduct				71	-0.099	74	-0.139	83	-0.185	83	-0.065	88	-0.366**	89	-0.145
Child's Peer Rating															
Reading				60	-0.040					78	-0.230			91	-0.203
Arithmetic				60	-0.094					78	-0.163			91	-0.270
Conduct				60	-0.115					78	-0.250			91	-0.227

Table 4.12
Continued

Standardized Achievement	Child's Sex†		First Grade PMA IQ		Second Grade SFTAA IQ	
	N	r	N	r	N	r
Reading	97	0.212	73	0.400**	83	0.468**
Arithmetic	97	0.107	73	0.335**	83	0.360**
Conduct	96	0.166	73	0.485**	83	0.494**

Standardized Achievement

Standardized Achievement	Reading		Arithmetic		Conduct	
	N	r	N	r	N	r
Reading	98	1.00	98	0.754**	97	0.823**
Arithmetic	98	0.754**	98	1.00	97	0.809**
Conduct	97	0.823**	97	0.809**	97	1.00

* Significant at the 0.05 level.
** Significant at the 0.01 level.
† Boys coded as 1, Girls codes as 2.

fluctuation is not obvious; teachers may get to know individual pupils better over the year and so become better at "partialling out" ability in their attempt to evaluate effort alone.

That teachers' marks consistently depend less on children's actual capabilities at year-end than at midyear provides support for the assertion that parents' expectations bring about change in children's marks (especially in first grade) by eliminating an alternative explanation. The reasoning is as follows. Imagine that parents' expectations strongly matched their children's ability whether ability was measured in general terms (IQ) or in more specific terms (standardized achievement), and that teachers, over the year, became better acquainted with children's ability. Imagine, further, that teachers, contrary to school policy, used ability information in assigning marks. The net effect of this set of propositions would be for children's marks to move toward parental expectations because of increased teacher sensitivity to ability rather than because of the causal impact of parents' expectations. Though a reasonable hypothesis and one partially supported by moderate IQ-parent expectation correlations and weak IQ-mark correlation changes within first grade (and only first grade), this hypothesis is quite untenable given that the regular fluctuations in the correlations between marks and standardized achievement are exactly opposite to those needed to confirm the hypothesis.

In any case, the substantial correlations of standardized achievement with marks (around 0.50 for reading and arithmetic in second and third grades) suggest that, for reading and arithmetic, children's performance as rated by teachers' marks probably can be generalized to children's performance measured on standardized tests. This fortunate outcome means that findings reported for children's marks probably apply to standardized test scores as well.

Table 4.12 shows that parents' expectations in each grade correlate to a significant degree with children's standardized test performance and that they are more strongly related to the level of the child's performance than are the child's own expectations. The longterm forecasting ability of parents is impressive. Before children get their first report card (time 1) parents display some ability to predict objective test scores in reading and arithmetic given in third grade. By the middle of second grade, after having seen four report cards, parents' forecasts for the academic areas correlate better with achievement scores than do IQ-test scores obtained later in second grade! Furthermore, the causal interplay between children's expectations and performance has produced a convergence between their expectations and their standardized achievement score. We see in the third-grade data sizeable, highly significant correlations between the children's own expectations and their actual performance for the first time in the core areas of reading and arithmetic.

Achievement with IQ Controlled

The reader will recall that the correlations between IQ and marks in reading or arithmetic were generally small (exceeding 0.3 in only one instance, arithmetic at midyear second grade), and that the correlations of IQ with children's expectations were even smaller in the first two grades. In second grade, for the first time to any impressive degree, there was significant matching between children's expectations and marks in conduct at midyear and significant matching between children's expectations and marks in all three subjects at year-end. Table 4.13 contains the correlations between children's expectations and their marks and between children's expectations and standardized achievement scores (measured in third grade) where both correlations have had IQ partialled out. Given the relatively small correlations with IQ, it is not surprising that children's expectations for themselves remain about as strongly correlated with marks when IQ is controlled as when it is not. (The zero-order and partial correlations for times 3 and 4 respectively are -0.073 vs. -0.075, 0.252 vs. 0.177, 0.315 vs. 0.301; 0.474 vs. 0.479, 0.511 vs. 0.516, and 0.309 vs. 0.309.) Clearly, IQ does not account for any substantial part of the correlation between children's marks and their expectations.

The pattern of stronger year-end mark-expectation correlations persists even with IQ controlled and, indeed, continues on into third grade. The same is true for the standardized-achievement-expectation correlations. There are stronger *midyear* correlations between marks and standardized achievement, however (table 4.12). The periodicity of these correlations warrants a continuation of the clear distinction between the causal relations present within and between years.

IQ plays a much larger role for standardized achievement than it did for marks (see table 4.12, where correlations of about 0.45 are reported). IQ, however, is still largely uncorrelated with children's expectations, so controlling IQ does not lead to large reductions in the correlation between standardized achievement and children's expectations, as can be seen from the appropriate sections of tables 4.12 and 4.13. (Some of the differences that appear may be attributed to the reduced case base present in table 4.13, a result of the list-wise deletion of cases used during the calculation of the partial correlations.)

By way of a general conclusion, then, we can say that controlling IQ does not substantially affect the correlation between children's expectations and their standardized achievement scores or the correlation between children's expectations and their marks. The small correlations between IQ and expectations form the feature that renders the control of IQ largely ineffective on the magnitude of the expectation-performance correlations. The magnitude of the correlations between expectations and standardized

Table 4.13

Correlations of Standardized Achievement Test Scores (Third Grade) and
Marks with Other Measures When IQ Is Controlled
Middle-Class School, Cohort S-1
(Listwise Deletion of Cases)

PMA IQ is used for grade one controls, SFTAA IQ is used for grade two and three controls

	Time 1		Time 2		Time 3		Time 4		Time 5		Time 6	
	N	r	N	r	N	r	N	r	N	r	N	r
Partial Correlations for Marks and Children's Expectations												
Reading	79	-0.005	81	0.198	95	-0.075	99	0.479**	81	0.127	81	0.306**
Arithmetic	79	0.092	81	0.205	96	0.177	99	0.516**	87	0.225*	87	0.456**
Conduct	79	0.166	81	0.316**	96	0.301**	99	0.309**	87	0.291**	87	0.456**
Partial Correlations for Standardized Achievement Scores (Gr. 3) and Children's Expectations												
Reading	71	0.025	71	-0.150	77	-0.059	82	-0.442**	78	-0.296*	78	-0.460**
Arithmetic	71	-0.258*	71	-0.252*	77	-0.170	82	-0.188	78	-0.395**	78	-0.458**
Conduct	71	-0.204	71	-0.138	77	-0.150	82	-0.173	78	0.039	78	-0.034
Partial Correlation for Standardized Achievement Scores (Gr. 3) and Parents' Expectations												
Reading	66	-0.227			59	-0.637**			67	-0.688**		
Arithmetic	66	-0.138			59	-0.323*			67	-0.487**		
Conduct	62	0.153			59	-0.172			67	-0.249*		

* Significant at the 0.05 level
** Significant at the 0.01 level

Table 4.14

Correlations between Peer Rating and Other Measures
Middle-Class School, Cohort S-1 in Second Grade

N = 98

Mean = 0.488

S.D. = 0.302

	N	r
Parent's Expectation--Midyear		
Reading	68	0.137
Arithmetic	67	0.227
Conduct	68	0.135
Child's Expectation--Midyear		
Reading	91	0.042
Arithmetic	91	0.056
Conduct	91	-0.015
Child's Expectation--Year-End		
Reading	94	0.121
Arithmetic	94	0.128
Conduct	94	0.130
Child's Mark--Midyear		
Reading	95	0.283**
Arithmetic	96	0.160
Conduct	96	0.175
Child's Mark--Year-End		
Reading	96	0.223*
Arithmetic	96	0.292**
Conduct	96	0.098
Sociometric Rating--Grade One	64	0.154
IQ (SFTAA)	95	0.053

* = significant at the .05 level.

** = significant at the .01 level.

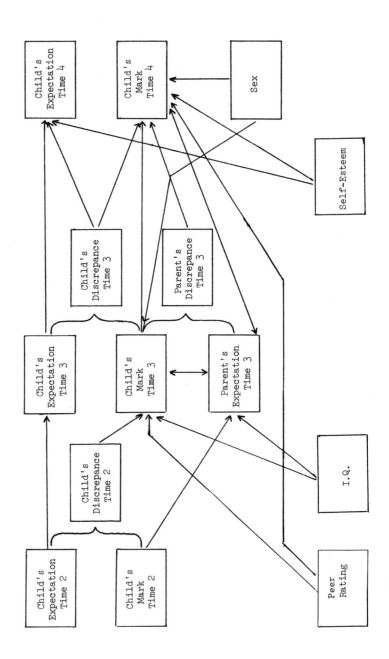

Figure 4.1

Reading Model, Middle-Class School, Second Grade

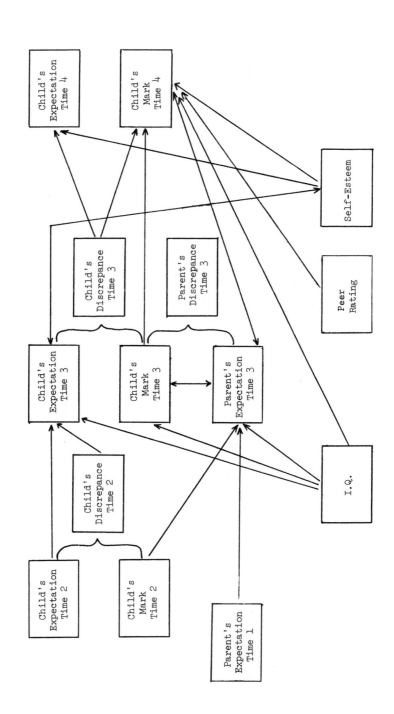

Figure 4.2

Arithmetic Model, Middle-Class School, Second Grade

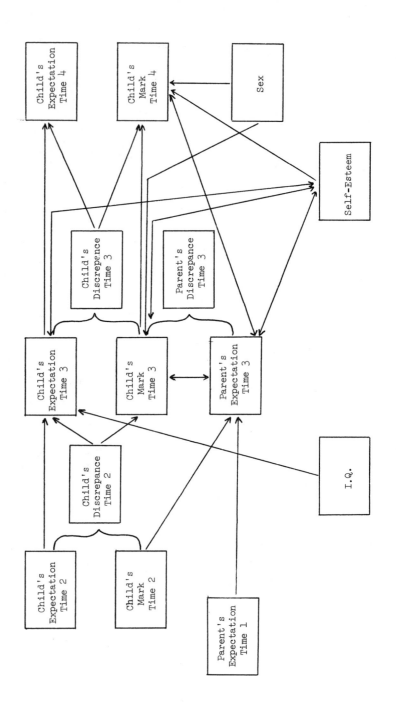

Figure 4.3
Conduct Model, Middle-Class School, Second Grade

achievement is impressive and, furthermore, suggests that these middle-class children are reasonably good judges of their own competence by the time they reach third grade.

Peer Ratings

The relationships displayed by the children's within-class peer ratings in second grade are largely similar to those for first grade (see table 4.14). Children's expectations remain unrelated to their peer rating, while their academic area marks remain slightly (yet significantly in three of four cases) related to the peer rating. The correlations with reading marks are probably artifacts of the testing procedure used (see the discussion of first-grade data). In all three areas, high standing with peers is associated with high marks.

Summary

Major findings for the three performance areas, again presented by way of visual models (figures 4.1, 4.2, and 4.3), deserve qualifiers similar to those voiced in the summary of chapter 3. Some specific points about these figures require clarification. First, some two-headed arrows appear despite definable time sequences (for example, figure 4.1, parent's time 3 expectations), because the existence of a direct effect is in some doubt. Other variables, whether or not in the diagram, may be involved in producing a spurious relationship in these cases. Second, within any one time unit no relationships are drawn between children's expectations and marks despite significant matching, because these relationships are conceived not as direct or reciprocal effects but, rather, as relations resulting from other diagrammed effects. Finally, some conditional effects are diagrammed; most notably, the self-esteem and IQ relations are often sex-specific in figure 4.3.

CHAPTER 5

Working-Class Children in First Grade

This chapter's focus is on another school, one in an urban setting. Its clientele is much lower in socioeconomic status than was the clientele of the middle-class school. Most importantly, the school enrolls a majority of black students (60%) rather than enrolling only white students, as did the middle-class school. We are interested here in all the questions that occupied our attention in chapters 3 and 4—what expectations children have when they start school, how these expectations change, what they influence and what they are influenced by—and, in addition, we are interested in whether the results differ along racial lines. We discovered that there were remarkably few differences associated with race, and those that emerged pertained mainly to parents.

In preceding chapters we saw that middle-class children start school with high expectations—too high, on the average. By the end of second grade, however, there is a significant consistency between children's expectations and their marks. We have also seen that teachers' marks and standardized test scores for these children are closely related, indicating that inferences about marks can be applied to the children's objectively measured performance in reading and/or arithmetic. We saw, furthermore, that children in the middle-class school performed well-above-grade level by the time Iowa scores became available. The high expectations of these children, therefore, tended to be borne out.

In this chapter we investigate development over a similar but shorter time period for children from less favored home backgrounds. The IQ of these lower-class children at the time they started school was somewhat above average, and the facilities of the school and its staff are at least equal to those of the middle-class school. Despite this comparability of opportunity and talent, however, by the time the reading skills of these children were assessed objectively, the children's level of performance was clearly below-grade level. How did this happen? What brought it about? We eventually address these questions directly. First, however, we present findings for the lower-class two-race school that parallel those already presented for the middle-class school.

Some of the findings about children's expectations are replicated with this new sample of children—the same paradoxical mismatch occurs between expectations in reading and arithmetic, for example. Such replication increases one's general confidence in all the findings. Interesting differences also occur in terms of significant others' and parents' influences. Parents are both less accurate and less influential, and peers are more influential.

Presentation of results for the integrated school occupies the remainder of this chapter. Contrasts or similarities to earlier findings are noted in passing, but a full-blown comparison of the two schools is presented in chapter 6.

Overview

The working-class school is located in a heavily populated urban area and is approximately the same size as the middle-class school. All first graders who started there in September 1972 were followed through the first grade. They form cohort L-1. Of the four classes of first graders that year, two were taught by black teachers and two were taught by white teachers. The student-body was 60% black and 40% white. (The few orientals present were classed as white.)

Data for the entire cohort, with separate summaries for its black and white members, are given in table 5.1. The working-class children in cohort L-1 were exceedingly optimistic about reading and conduct before their first report card. Their expectations for reading and conduct were significantly higher than their expectations for arithmetic ($p < .01$ for both paired t-tests), but even for arithmetic they expected more than a B, on the average (1.74). Children's average expectations in all three areas remained remarkably stable over the first-grade year.

Interviewers obtained expectations from 74% of the working-class parents—again, it was usually the child's mother (97%). In advance of the interviewer's call, a note was sent home with the child, explaining to the parents that an interviewer would come to the home a day or two hence. The note explained the purpose of the interview and reassured the parent that the reason for the visit was not that the child was in difficulty. As many as three call-backs were used to try to reach parents. A black interviewer went to see black parents and a white interviewer went to see white parents. Even with three call-backs fewer working-class parents than middle-class parents were contacted.

Working-class parents' expectations in all three subjects were much lower than their children's expectations (significant beyond the .01 level for reading, arithmetic, and conduct).

Table 5.1

Means, Standard Deviations for First-Grade Cohort
Working-Class School, 60% Black

	Black			White			Combined		
	N	Mean	S.D.	N	Mean	S.D.	N	Mean	S.D.
IQ--PMA	77	101.4	12.5	52	106.2	15.1	130	103.3	13.7
Parent's Expectation--Midyear									
Reading	62	2.37	0.77	43	2.28	0.85	105	2.33	0.81
Arithmetic	62	2.15	0.74	44	2.34	0.78	106	2.23	0.76
Conduct	62	2.08	0.49	44	1.61	0.62	106	1.89	0.59
Child's Expectation--Midyear									
Reading	68	1.28	0.62	43	1.26	0.49	113	1.28	0.59
Arithmetic	68	1.65	0.48	43	1.88	0.76	113	1.74	0.62
Conduct	68	1.07	0.26	43	1.07	0.26	113	1.07	0.26
Child's Expectation--Year-End									
Reading	71	1.28	0.59	47	1.32	0.76	119	1.32	0.70
Arithmetic	71	1.75	0.82	48	1.77	0.81	120	1.75	0.81
Conduct	71	1.24	0.49	48	1.23	0.56	120	1.23	0.51
Child's Mark--Midyear									
Reading	43[a]	3.16	0.84	29	3.14	0.88	72	3.15	0.85
Arithmetic	76	3.09	0.77	52	2.92	0.71	129	3.03	0.75
Conduct	76	2.03	0.61	52	1.77	0.58	129	1.93	0.62
Child's Mark--Year-End									
Reading	78	2.69	0.90	49	2.43	0.84	127	2.59	0.89
Arithmetic	78	2.89	0.99	49	2.59	0.91	127	2.77	0.97
Conduct	78	1.81	0.74	49	1.59	0.71	127	1.72	0.73

[a]One teacher did not give marks in reading on the first report card.

Table 5.1 (Continued)

Summary of Changes over School Year, First Grade, Cohort L-1

	Black			White			Combined		
	N	Mean	S.D.	N	Mean	S.D.	N	Mean	S.D.
Mark Change (Midyear Mark minus Year-End Mark)[a]									
Reading	43	0.63	0.62	26	0.81	0.63	69	0.70	0.63
Arithmetic	74	0.18	0.73	47	0.30	0.75	121	0.22	0.74
Conduct	74	0.22	0.71	47	0.19	0.65	121	0.21	0.68
Expectation Change (Midyear Expectation minus Year-End Expectation)									
Reading	61	0.00	0.82	36	-0.11	0.98	98	-0.05	0.88
Arithmetic	61	-0.13	0.90	37	0.03	0.99	99	-0.06	0.94
Conduct	61	-0.18	0.50	37	-0.22	0.67	99	-0.19	0.57
Midyear Mark-Expectation Discrepancy (Midyear Mark minus Midyear Expectation)									
Reading	39[a]	1.77	1.04	22	1.96	1.05	61	1.84	1.04
Arithmetic	66	1.41	0.86	42	1.10	0.73	109	1.30	0.83
Conduct	66	0.92	0.62	42	0.69	0.47	109	0.84	0.58
Year-End Mark-Expectation Discrepancy (Year-End Mark minus Year-End Expectation)									
Reading	69	1.38	0.99	46	1.00	1.08	116	1.23	1.03
Arithmetic	69	1.09	1.25	47	0.75	1.19	117	0.97	1.24
Conduct	69	0.54	0.83	47	0.32	0.78	117	0.45	0.82

[a]Footnote on p. 1 of table.

Teachers in this school gave marks based on grade-level norms,* not on "effort," as was true in the middle-class school. Thus a child in this school who read at second-grade level in first grade would get a "1," and a child who did not attain grade level, say, one who read only at the pre-primer level at the end of first grade, would get a "4," regardless of the effort he displayed.

Children's average marks on the first report card in this school were very low, below C in reading and arithmetic. Children's marks did improve significantly ($p < .01$) in all three areas over the first-grade year, however, with the largest improvement in reading (0.56), but in no case did marks come close to the children's initial expectation level. Children's expectations were, thus, strikingly violated—the marks children received were far different from their expectations at any time.

First marks were also considerably lower than parents had expected, even though parents expected much less than their children did. Even after considerable improvement over the year, the marks remained lower than the parents had forecast in November.

There were 57 white children and 86 black children in cohort L-1. Before receiving their first report card, children of both races were highly optimistic about their forthcoming marks in reading and in conduct, but noticeably less optimistic about their forthcoming marks in arithmetic. Whites estimated an arithmetic mark 0.23 units lower than blacks, but the average difference was not significant. Children's average expectations over the year remained rather constant, regardless of the race of the child.

Expectations were obtained from 77% of white children's parents and 72% of black children's parents. White parents and black parents have comparable expectations for their first-grade children except in conduct, where white parents looked for a significantly better mark (1.61 vs. 2.08, $p < .01$). Note, however, that, on the average, both the black and the white parents expected conduct marks not far from a B. Parents' expectations were uniformly lower than their children's expectations within both racial groups.

On the average, children of the two races actually attained marks that

---

*Reading marks are harder to evaluate than marks in arithmetic or conduct because the different teachers used different marking schemes—each assigned marks related to the read-ing book series she used in her classroom, and three different reading book series (Distar, Bookmark, and Primer) were used. Two of the series employ the same letters to indicate the difficulty of reading books, but the same letters designate *different* levels in the two series. "P" in one system, for example, means a higher mark than "P" in the other. The system of marking reading was confusing to teachers, researchers, and, probably most of all, to chil-dren. For this research reading marks were coded on a 1 to 4 numerical scale like that used for coding marks in the other subjects, by judging as closely as possible what the equivalence should be between the letter and number designations.

were very close, although white children's marks over the first-grade year improved a little more than blacks' in both reading and arithmetic. Except for this small differential improvement over the year, differences between black and white children on all the measures listed in table 5.1 are negligible. Therefore, with a few exceptions, differences between races will be ignored in presenting the major findings for cohort L-1 and in contrasting these findings with those previously presented for middle-class children. Later in this chapter, in a separate section on racial differences, we summarize the few findings significantly associated with race.

The average IQ in the working-class school at first grade (103, N = 130) is somewhat lower than the average IQ of middle-class first graders (114). (Both groups received the Primary Mental Abilities test.) This difference, although significant, must be weighed against the difference between years for cohort S-1 of the middle-class school. Recall that their IQ scores averaged 115 in first grade compared to 104 in second grade. The IQ difference *between* schools (L-1 vs S-1+2) is about as large as the difference *within* one cohort (S-1) as it passed from first to second grade and was retested. (Note that different tests—PMA and SFTAA—are also involved in the comparison between grades for cohort S-1.) The true interschool differences in IQ, therefore, may be less significant than would be estimated looking only at the first-grade IQ scores. In any case, both schools enroll children whose IQ's are above average.

In cohort L-1 the correlations between IQ and marks are substantial in every case, unlike our findings for the middle-class school. These correlations (table 5.2) must be evaluated with an eye to the manner in which marks are assigned in the working-class school. The report card that these children take home says: "Your child's progress is being measured in terms of his progress in reaching standards or levels that are considered appropriate for his age or years in school." Marking is, thus, in terms of grade-level performance, comparing the child's progress with the average progress of children his age. (Children in the middle-class school were marked in terms of how hard they tried, independent of their ability.) The highly significant and substantial correlations between IQ and marks in both reading and arithmetic throughout first grade and the consistency of these correlations within both the black and white subsamples demonstrate that teachers were fairly successful in carrying out this marking policy.

Conduct marks were significantly correlated with IQ at both midyear and year-end, but this relationship is largely confined to the white portion of the cohort. There were consistently larger conduct-IQ correlations for whites than for blacks (high IQ being associated with good marks). Indeed, at year-end the correlation for blacks is almost zero, while the correlation for whites approaches that observed for reading and arithmetic.

Table 5.2

Correlations between IQ (PMA) and Other Measures
Working-Class School, First Grade

	Black Only		White Only		Combined Races	
	Mean = 101.4		Mean = 106.2		Mean = 103.3	
	S.D. = 12.4		S.D. = 15.1		S.D. = 13.7	
	$\underline{N}$	$\underline{r}$	$\underline{N}$	$\underline{r}$	$\underline{N}$	$\underline{r}$
Parent's Expectation--Midyear (T1)						
Reading	62	-0.209	43	-0.498**	105	-0.349**
Arithmetic	62	-0.174	44	-0.591**	106	-0.339**
Conduct	62	-0.049	44	-0.339*	106	-0.240*
Child's Expectation--Midyear (T1)						
Reading	65	0.042	39	-0.002	104	0.020
Arithmetic	65	-0.112	39	-0.258	104	-0.152
Conduct	65	0.091	39	-0.176	104	-0.021
Child's Expectation--Year-End (T2)						
Reading	71	-0.300*	46	0.086	117	-0.109
Arithmetic	71	-0.115	47	-0.030	118	-0.078
Conduct	71	0.011	47	-0.118	118	-0.054
Child's Mark--Midyear (T1)						
Reading	43	-0.500**	28	-0.302	71	-0.411**
Arithmetic	73	-0.525**	48	-0.388**	121	-0.476**
Conduct	73	-0.157	48	-0.275	121	-0.236**
Child's Mark--Year-End (T2)						
Reading	76	-0.462**	48	-0.494**	124	-0.484**
Arithmetic	76	-0.401**	48	-0.436**	124	-0.427**
Conduct	76	-0.006	48	-0.406**	124	-0.191*

---

* = significant at the .05 level.

** = significant at the .01 level.

Correlations are negligible between children's expectations and IQ, and the two races are rather similar in this respect, with the exception that black children register a significant year-end correlation between IQ and reading expectations and whites do not. There is no obvious explanation for this isolated finding.

The significant correlations between IQ and parents' first expectations for the combined races mask effects noted when the races are examined separately. One of the most provocative findings in this entire study is that white parents' expectations in all three areas are significantly and fairly strongly correlated with IQ, and that the correlations for black parents are consistently weak and nonsignificant (table 5.2). White working-class parents (like white middle-class parents) apparently are either attuned to the cues that indicate their child's IQ and/or more readily utilize these cues in forming their expectations. The children, whether white or black, and black parents seem oblivious to IQ in shaping their expectations.

This startling difference between working-class parents of the two races was unexpected; it could have profound significance for the academic socialization of children of the two races. It may signify that previous feedback about children's performance has not been processed by the black parents or is processed differently by white and black parents. If both black parents and black children continue to ignore cues related to IQ in producing their academic forecasts, there may be little constructive use of feedback. On the other hand, if they begin to incorporate *mark* feedback into the formation of their expectations, they will be incorporating something of IQ, since IQ and marks are fairly consistently correlated in the working-class school, at least in first grade.

Correspondence between Expectations and Marks

Data indicating that expectations of children in the working-class school far outstripped the marks they received are these: not a single student got a mark that exceeded his expectation in reading at midyear first grade, and only 10% of the students were able to meet their expectations. Furthermore, a large percentage of those who received the lowest possible mark in reading (21 out of 26, or 81%) expected the highest mark. The picture is just as bleak for arithmetic and conduct, even though expectations for arithmetic are lower (table 5.3). In no area do children's midyear expectations and marks match one another to a significant degree.

Since teachers gave no reading marks equivalent to A's, the reader may wonder whether our recoding of letter marks to numerical marks was faulty and whether we should have shifted the whole numerical scale one position lower. We strongly doubt it. Both the teachers' comments on students' report cards and the levels of student competence normally associated with the letter grades assigned indicate that teachers did view the students' level of competence as being markedly skewed toward the low end.

Table 5.3

Joint Distribution of Working-Class Children's Expectations and Marks, First Report Card

(Percentages, N = 60 for Reading[*], 108 for Arithmetic and Conduct)

Marks, Midyear

	Reading					Arithmetic					Conduct			
Expectation, Midyear	1	2	3	4	Total	1	2	3	4	Total	1	2	3	Total
1	0.0	16.7	21.7	35.0	73.3	0.9	14.8	11.1	8.3	35.2	20.4	62.0	10.2	92.6
2	0.0	8.3	8.3	5.0	21.7	0.0	8.3	34.3	17.6	60.2	0.0	5.6	1.9	7.4
3	0.0	0.0	1.7	3.3	5.0	0.0	0.9	0.9	0.9	2.8	0.0	0.0	0.0	0.0
4	0.0	0.0	0.0	0.0	0.0	0.0	0.0	0.0	1.9	1.9	0.0	0.0	0.0	0.0
Total	0.0	25.0	31.7	43.3	100.0	0.9	24.1	46.3	28.7	100.0	20.4	67.6	12.0	100.0

[*]One class was not assigned midyear reading marks.

Even with the very low marks at midyear, almost all the children continued to hold high expectations at year-end. The large discrepance between the children's initial expectations and their first marks apparently had little impact. There was substantial (but not statistically significant) consistency in the children's expectations over the year (68%, 42%, and 77% of the expectations matched in reading, arithmetic, and conduct, respectively), but none of these values is significant because of the skew in the expectation distributions (table 5.4).

Chance levels of matching between children's expectations and marks prevailed in all three areas at year-end, continuing the general pattern observed at midyear.

As was true in the middle-class school, initial marks in reading and arithmetic showed more consistency (53%) than would be expected by chance (31%) ($z = 4.04$, $p < .01$)—teachers tended to be consistent in the marks they assigned in the two subjects. By the end of the year the agreement between marks in the two areas increased to 58%, exceeding chance (29%) by an even greater margin that was true at midyear ($z = 7.60$, $p < .001$). At the end of the year there was also a significant matching between arithmetic and conduct marks—the only agreement conduct marks displayed with other marks during the year.

We see again in this school the paradox noted in the middle-class school: teachers tended to give similar marks in reading and arithmetic, but children's expectations for the two areas were not similar. At midyear there was significantly less agreement between children's expectations for reading and arithmetic (28%) than would be predicted by chance (37%) ($z = -2.29$, $p < .05$), and at the end of the year the matching between reading and arithmetic expectations (36%) continued to be less than chance would predict (41%), although not significantly less ($z = -1.45$).

This finding deserves careful attention. The fact that there is significantly less consistency than chance would predict in two different schools and that the undermatching is in a direction opposite to teachers' behavior argues strongly for the internal validity of the expectation measure: for some reason those children who expect to do well in reading are less optimistic about arithmetic, and vice versa.

Despite the significant improvement in children's marks in all three areas over the year, there was also a persistence in marks over the year—a phenomenon also seen in the middle-class school. In all three areas, significantly more marks were the same at both midyear and year-end than would be expected by chance (39%, 54%, and 50%, respectively for reading, arithmetic, and conduct), but the marks that did change showed predominantly upward movement.

Table 5.4

Joint Distribution of Working-Class Children's Expectations at Midyear and Year-End, First Grade

(Percentages, N = 95 for Reading; N = 96 for Arithmetic and Conduct)

		Reading					Arithmetic					Conduct				
		1	2	3	4	Total	1	2	3	4	Total	1	2	3	4	Total
Expectation, Midyear	1	64.2	9.5	3.2	2.1	79.0	17.7	13.5	5.2	0.0	36.5	76.0	15.6	1.0	1.0	93.8
	2	11.6	4.2	0.0	1.1	16.8	26.0	24.0	6.3	4.2	60.4	4.2	1.0	1.0	0.0	6.3
	3	2.1	1.1	0.0	0.0	3.2	0.0	3.1	0.0	0.0	3.1	0.0	0.0	0.0	0.0	0.0
	4	1.1	0.0	0.0	0.0	1.1	0.0	0.0	0.0	0.0	0.0	0.0	0.0	0.0	0.0	0.0
	Total	79.0	14.7	3.2	3.2	100.0	43.8	40.6	11.5	4.2	100.0	80.2	16.7	2.1	1.0	100.0

Expectation, Year-End

The Effects of Feedback

For the working-class school as for the middle-class school, several analyses too extensive to present in detail were pursued to test various hypotheses that might explain changes observed in marks and expectations over the year. For cohort L-1 these analyses are less complete than are those for the combined S-1 and S-2 cohorts presented in chapter 3, because the case base for L-1 is smaller, and also because the narrow variance in children's expectations in cohort L-1 reduces the power of tests. Nevertheless, insofar as analysis was possible, the findings here are the same as for the middle-class school.

It is almost meaningless to examine whether children pay differential attention to marks in forming their expectations, because the preponderant combination of exceedingly high children's expectations with low marks severely restricts possible patterns of outcomes. The extreme discrepances between children's expectations and marks suggest that the children generally pay little attention to actual performance in forming their expectations. Why else would children's expectations be so unrealistically high? For the data most amenable to analysis—that of arithmetic at year-end—no matter what initial marks children received, they all tended to voice the same kinds of high expectations. The lack of correspondence between midyear marks and year-end expectations replicates the findings for middle-class children.

A second question is whether children of differing expectation levels differ in their ability to form realistic expectations. The only data that permit analysis of this question, again, are data for arithmetic at year-end. There is no suggestion that any particular expectation level is more closely associated with realistic expectations than any other level, replicating what was found with more extensive analyses for middle-class children.

We now turn to a consideration of how the child's expectation-mark discrepance at midyear affected change over the first-grade year. Again, the analysis of expectation-mark discrepances can not be as thorough as the parallel analyses for the middle-class school, but available results *are* consistent with the findings for middle-class children. Over-the-year movement in either marks or expectations, when it occurred, tended to be in the direction of increasing the consistency between expectations and marks. In all three sets of marks, children whose marks improved tended to be those whose marks earlier were less than they expected, but those whose marks declined also tended to be those whose marks earlier were less than they expected, simply because most of the children received marks lower than they expected at midyear. However, in arithmetic and conduct, significantly more students tended to show an improvement in their marks (as opposed to showing a decline) when there was an earlier discrepance of the type where the child's midyear mark was less than expected, compared to the improvements and declines that followed no discrepance (tables 5.5 and 5.6). Too few cases with no discrepance are available in reading for the hypothesis to be effectively tested, however.

For changes in expectations, the data for reading are, again, too constrained to test for movement toward consistency. The data for arithmetic expectations do not show a significant movement toward consistency, while the data for conduct display a significant downward shift for those who did worse than expected at midyear.

In contrast with the middle-class school, there is no buoyancy effect for working-class children's expectations. However, the data are few, so a robust test of the hypothesis remains to be made, and the ceiling imposed by the extraordinarily high initial level of children's expectations also militates against a satisfactory test. In short, data for mark changes (including the nonsignificant trends) bear out the findings for middle-class children insofar as the same trends can display themselves, but data for expectation changes are in only partial agreement with middle-class data. There is a little movement toward consistency in expectations, but the buoyancy effect is absent.

Why did low marks at midyear have almost no effect on working-class children's expectations at year-end? Perhaps children do not know how they have been evaluated. The report card marks in reading were hard for anyone to interpret, as mentioned earlier. None of the marking schemes for reading coincided with the codes for other subjects on the report card (A, B, C, D or 1, 2, 3, 4). What children were processing as feedback, therefore, may have depended very little on report card marks in reading, perhaps causing the children to rely almost exclusively on the informal evaluations their teachers gave during daily classroom instruction.

The Distar Program, interestingly enough, which was in use in two of the four classrooms under study in cohort L-1, emphasizes lavish use of positive reinforcement: the teacher congratulates the child by shaking his hand, giving him raisins or other small pieces of food, and pinning signs on him such as "I read today," as well as by supplying the more usual types of reinforcement, like a steady flow of verbal praise and smiles. This exaggerated kind of daily positive feedback may kindle very high expectations in children, high enough to swamp the formal (negative) feedback from report cards.

Encouragement and positive feedback are certainly necessary to motivate children in day-to-day classroom efforts. One wonders, though, what effect the extreme dissonance between the teacher's classroom behavior and her forced use of an absolute marking scale, as in the working-

Table 5.5

Changes in Arithmetic over First Grade
as a Function of the Expectation-Mark Discrepance at Midyear
Working-Class School
(Predicted and Observed Frequencies)

Changes in Arithmetic Marks, T1 to T2

| | | Up | | Same | | Down | | |
		Pred.	Obs.	Pred.	Obs.	Pred.	Obs.	Total
Child Previously	Better	0	0	1	1	0	0	1
Did B,S,W Than	Same	4	2	6	5	2	5	12
He Expected (T1)	Worse	32	35	45	46	11	8	89
	Total		37		52		13	102

Changes in Arithmetic Expectations, T1 to T2

| | | Up | | Same | | Down | | |
		Pred.	Obs.	Pred.	Obs.	Pred.	Obs.	Total
Child Previously	Better	0	1	0	0	0	0	1
Did B,S,W Than	Same	3	5	5	4	3	2	11
He Expected (T1)	Worse	25	22	35	36	25	26	84
	Total		28		40		28	96

class school, may eventually have. What happens to the child, for example, when later, in the second or third grade, he looks back upon a long series of low marks and realizes what earlier report cards actually signified?

While the unintelligibility of marking schemes may account for the lack of a feedback effect in reading, the lack of feedback effects in arithmetic and conduct cannot be dismissed on the same grounds. Here one plausible explanation for the lack of effect is that informal positive feedback given by the teacher in daily classroom sessions outweighs the infrequent negative feedback on report cards. Another plausible explanation is that

Table 5.6

Changes in Conduct over First Grade
as a Function of the Expectation-Mark Discrepance at Midyear
Working-Class School
(Predicted and Observed Frequencies)

Changes in Conduct Marks, T1 to T2

		Up		Same		Down		
		Pred.	Obs.	Pred.	Obs.	Pred.	Obs.	Total
Child Previously	Same	10	3	13	19	4	5	27
Did S,W Than								
He Expected (T1)	Worse	27	34	37	31	11	10	75
	Total		37		50		15	102

Changes in Conduct Expectations, T1 to T2

		Up		Same		Down		
		Pred.	Obs.	Pred.	Obs.	Pred.	Obs.	Total
Child Previously	Same	1	3	19	17	5	5	25
Did S,W Than								
He Expected (T1)	Worse	3	1	55	57	13	13	71
	Total		4		74		18	96

persons who are the targets of low evaluations do not perceive the evaluator to be dissatisfied as often as the evaluator actually is dissatisfied (as in Dornbusch and Scott's 1975:171 finding for school teachers and principals).

Parents' Expectations

We saw that working-class parents had lower expectations than middle-class parents and that their expectations exceeded their children's performances. In all three areas, furthermore, there was no significant agreement between parents and children at the individual level. In the working-class school as in the middle-class school, parents and children expected different things.

In contrast to the middle-class school, where parents seemed aware of "marking norms," here parents were inaccurate at the aggregate level. Also in contrast to the middle-class school, there was little correspondence at the individual level between parents' expectations and the reading marks their children received on first report cards. Only 27% of the working-class parents' reading expectations were borne out (compared to 25% expected by chance). At the end of first grade, though, after marks improved, the amount of agreement between parents' reading expectations and marks went up to 52%, a highly significant amount compared to a chance prediction of 33% ($z = 4.42$, $p < .01$).

Why did parents' midyear expectations significantly match year-end reading marks but not midyear marks? The answer lies in the unusually low marks given for reading at midyear—improvement in marks was noted for 61% of the children over the year. The distributions of midyear reading marks and parent expectations were too different to allow substantial matching. Even at year-end, after a large majority of children had shown improvement, two-thirds of those parents whose expectations were off-target tended to overestimate ($\chi^2_1 = 4.50$, $p < .05$).

In arithmetic, at both midyear and year-end, the amount of agreement between parents' expectations and marks did not significantly exceed chance levels. (Marks in arithmetic rose less over the year than marks in reading did.) Only in conduct, a nonacademic area, did working-class parents' expectations match marks to an extent consistently above chance for the entire year.

Since parents' academic forecasts were not accurate, there is no need to investigate for working-class children what may produce parents' accuracy. Independent of the question of their accuracy, however, we may still ask what determined parents' expectations.

Like white middle-class parents, white working-class parents displayed a highly significant correlation between IQ and expectations for reading ($r = -.498$) and arithmetic ($r = -.591$). There was a smaller but still significant ($p < .05$) correlation between IQ and white parents' expectations for conduct ($r = -.339$). White working-class parents, to some substantial extent, then, based their expectations on their perception of their child's IQ. The absence of significant correlations between IQ and black parents' expectations suggests that IQ plays little part in the determination of these black working-class parents' initial expectations.

It is interesting that white working-class parents' expectations for reading and arithmetic are about as strongly correlated with their children's

IQ scores in first grade as white middle-class parents' expectations are. However, since working-class parents are generally poor at forecasting academic marks, the attempts of even white working-class parents to provide feedback for their children may be misguided. Expectations of parents and children do not coincide, but neither one is generally correct.

By his own inability to forecast, the parent of a working-class first grader may add to the confusion already created in the child's mind by the child's inability to forecast. The parent does not anticipate low marks, and so may be at a loss to interpret marks or to suggest how to go about improving them. The race differences in the correlations between IQ and parental expectations suggest that white parents may be more reliable and accurate sources of feedback than black parents, but the case base is not large enough for this notion to be pursued.

Despite the general inaccuracy of parental expectations, the effectiveness of parents' midyear mark-expectation discrepancies on the production of changes in children's marks over the first-grade year remains an issue. For the tables relating parents' midyear discrepancies to mark changes (tables similar to table 5.5), the minor diagonal is overrepresented in all three areas. The overrepresentation is significant, however, only for reading ($z = 1.76$, $p < .05$ one-sided; arithmetic, $z = 0.90$; conduct, $z = 1.51$). Reading, therefore, is the only area in which marks moved significantly toward consistency with parental expectations. This contrasts with the middle-class school, where the midyear parental discrepancy was effective in all three areas in first grade.

Sex Differences

First, as for the middle-class school, there are no differences in children's expectations by sex. Reading and arithmetic marks did not show association with sex at either midyear or year-end. but conduct marks showed the usual pattern of girls getting significantly better marks throughout the year.

Two sex differences emerge in terms of the sizes of the correlations between IQ and marks. For reading, the correlations for boys are slightly larger than for girls (table 5.7). The most interesting difference is that IQ is significantly—and strongly on first report card—correlated with boys' marks in conduct but not with girls' marks in conduct. This finding contrasts sharply with that noted for middle-class children. There, only girls' conduct marks were significantly correlated with IQ.

Parents, for the most part, expected boys and girls to do equally well in all three areas, and in no area was there significant agreement between

Table 5.7

Correlations between IQ and Marks by Sex
Working-Class School, First Grade

	Cohort L-1		
	N	Mean	S.D.
Both Sexes, IQ	130	103.3	13.7
Boys, IQ	62	104.7	14.0
Girls, IQ	68	102.0	13.5

	Correlations with IQ	
	N	r
Both Sexes' Marks--Midyear		
Reading	71	-0.411**
Arithmetic	121	-0.476**
Conduct	121	-0.236**
Both Sexes' Marks--Year-End		
Reading	124	-0.484**
Arithmetic	124	-0.427**
Conduct	124	-0.191*
Boys' Marks--Midyear		
Reading	33	-0.489**
Arithmetic	57	-0.564**
Conduct	57	-0.492**
Boys' Marks--Year-End		
Reading	60	-0.563**
Arithmetic	60	-0.404**
Conduct	60	-0.276*
Girls' Marks--Midyear		
Reading	38	-0.342*
Arithmetic	64	-0.443**
Conduct	64	-0.061
Girls' Marks--Year-End		
Reading	64	-0.422**
Arithmetic	64	-0.471**
Conduct	64	-0.225

* = significant at the .05 level.
** = significant at the .01 level.

what boys and their parents expected, or between what parents expected
and the marks boys got. Boys are apparently inscrutable to their parents!
For girls, the situation is a little better. Girls and their parents displayed
some agreement in their forecasts for reading marks, although, since
neither parents nor children forecast accurately, this agreement implies that
they both have similar, erroneous opinions. Parents can forecast girls'
conduct marks with some success.

Racial Differences

Perhaps the most interesting findings—or *non*-findings—in this chapter pertain to race. It should be reiterated that both blacks and whites have
close-to-average IQ scores—101 for blacks, 106 for whites. The minimal
differences associated with race in average parental and children's expectations were discussed briefly, earlier in this chapter, along with the data
presented in tables 5.1 and 5.2. The only substantial differences were that
white parents expected better conduct marks than black parents and that
only white parents' expectations were significantly correlated with IQ.

Black children and white children behaved almost identically in terms
of expectation levels when compared over the first year. Both races were
also similar in that the observed levels of matching between midyear and
year-end expectations did not differ from chance. Marks likewise showed
little association with race at either midyear or year-end.

In all areas, for both races, only a small amount of matching between
marks and expectations is expected, due to the skewed marginals. Observed matches do not differ significantly from these low expected values
for either race. The skewed marginals produce a strong asymmetry (expectations exceeding marks) in all areas for children of both races.

Children of the two races remained overly optimistic about reading
marks even after receiving low midyear marks. The percentage of children
holding a year-end reading expectation that is two or more points above the
midyear mark is 54% for whites and 68% for blacks. Since white children
received slightly but not significantly higher marks at midyear, these percentages are in line with the conclusion that whites and blacks are identical
in their adjustment of expectations to earlier marks. In arithmetic 31% of
whites and 48% of blacks hold a year-end expectation two or more points
above their midyear mark. Again, however, whites had received slightly
(but not significantly) better marks at midyear. Differences in assigned
marks are sufficient to account for differences in overoptimism between
races, and there seems to be no race differences in the response to first
marks.

There appear to be no special effects on either marks or expectations of children participating in classrooms where the teacher's race is the same as the child's race or in classrooms where the teacher's race is different from the child's race. Black and white teachers treated black students similarly. When black students were treated differently from white students—for example, blacks got lower midyear conduct marks—the lower marks are assigned equally by black and white teachers.

Literature on effects of integration, especially on the kinds of variables treated here, is scarce. This is particularly true for elementary-school children. On this account, it is noteworthy that first graders in an integrated working-class school differ very little by race. In other research in this same school on topics not reported in this volume, one of us (D.E.) has repeatedly observed this lack of racial differences. This school seems to be almost a textbook example of successful integration, a fact which makes the school especially interesting for a study of expectations.

What is there about this school that might foster such success? First, both the student body and staff have consisted of about equal numbers of blacks and whites *for a period of years.* Second, the school draws its clientele from mostly all-white or all-black city blocks, but blocks are intermingled and many interracial contacts occur in stores, in playgrounds, and in workplaces. Third, there have been a number of community efforts to spark citizen interest in the school and in the local neighborhoods. Fourth, specific attempts have been made to retain the same teachers in the school year after year and to maintain a racial balance of children in the school. Most impressive to the authors is the esprit de corps in the school—the staff is of very high quality and staff turnover is relatively low.

Peer Ratings

Relationships between within-classroom peer ratings and marks in both reading and arithmetic are highly significant for blacks at both midyear and year-end (table 5.8). The same relationships for whites are consistently smaller, with only one of the four attaining significance (midyear arithmetic mark, $p < .05$). For both marking periods whites manifest relationships between peer rating and conduct of the same size as those manifested for reading and arithmetic, and for first mark the correlation is large enough to attain significance. The positive relation between white children's peer rating and conduct marks contrasts with the findings for blacks, for whom no correlation is found at either time. The differences between races are so noticeable that consideration of the combined data for peer ratings seems inappropriate—trends seen there mask what is happening within groups.

It is particularly interesting that average peer ratings for whites and

Table 5.8

Correlations between Peer Rating and Other Measures
Working-Class School, First Grade

	Black Only N = 67		White Only N = 38		Combined Races N = 105	
	Mean = 0.489		Mean = 0.496		Mean = 0.492	
	S.D. = 0.308		S.D. = 0.286		S.D. = 0.299	
	N	r	N	r	N	r
Parent's Expectation--Midyear						
Reading	56	0.157	31	0.006	87	0.110
Arithmetic	56	0.237	32	-0.153	88	0.114
Conduct	56	0.011	32	0.169	88	0.037
Child's Expectation--Midyear						
Reading	61	-0.067	32	0.163	93	-0.013
Arithmetic	61	0.199	32	0.148	93	0.180
Conduct	61	-0.211	32	0.042	93	-0.140
Child's Expectation--Year-End						
Reading	60	-0.002	34	0.233	94	0.101
Arithmetic	60	0.123	35	0.234	95	0.162
Conduct	60	-0.175	35	0.119	95	-0.056
Child's Mark--Midyear						
Reading	40	0.454**	19	0.360	59	0.435**
Arithmetic	63	0.480**	37	0.353*	100	0.433**
Conduct	63	-0.004	37	0.360*	100	0.114
Child's Mark--Year-End						
Reading	64	0.456**	35	0.246	99	0.383**
Arithmetic	64	0.472**	35	0.333	99	0.419**
Conduct	64	-0.006	35	0.288	99	0.090

* = significant at the .05 level.
** = significant at the .01 level.

blacks are virtually identical, 0.489 for blacks and 0.496 for whites. In the eyes of their classmates, the popularity or perceived academic standing of children of both races is the same, but there seems to be more concordance between how classmates and how teachers perceive black children's performance in reading and arithmetic. It has frequently been speculated that whites have stronger achievement needs and blacks have stronger affiliation needs. Although these data do not test such an hypothesis directly, they are consistent with the kinds of relationships one would look for if that hypothesis were true. If the hypothesis held true, one would expect popular white children to behave in line with teachers' wishes (good conduct) to enhance achievement goals, whereas blacks would ignore teachers' wishes in an attempt to score points with their peers.

In no case does peer rating correlate significantly with either black or white children's expectations for themselves or with either black or white parents' expectations for their children. There is a significant ($p < .05$) but relatively small correlation between IQ and peer rating, however, ($r = -0.214$, $N = 98$), indicating that brighter children are more popular. (This finding parallels that for the middle-class white school.)

There are three significant correlations between peer rating and the amount by which expectations exceed performance (the expectation-mark discrepance). Again, as was true in the middle-class school, overoptimism seems weakly but significantly associated with unpopularity.

With IQ partialled out, slightly smaller but still highly significant correlations remain between peer rating and children's first-grade reading and arithmetic marks in the working-class school (see the combined section of table 5.9). The negligible correlations between peer rating and first-grade conduct marks persist when IQ is partialled out. The absence of substantial change in the mark-peer-rating correlation for the white cohort when IQ is controlled is deceptive, however, since the black and white subsamples behaved somewhat differently in the peer rating relationships they displayed (see table 5.8). In particular, the white subsample displayed smaller and less significant correlations with academic area marks and larger and more significant relationships with conduct marks.

When IQ is controlled, all the mark-peer-rating correlations for the white subsample increase, while the correlations for the black subsample decrease. After partialling, the white and black subsamples are more similar in terms of substantive area mark-peer-rating correlations than they were before partialling, with three of the four correlations significant in both groups and the general magnitude of the correlations more comparable. The race differences for conduct, however, remain as pronounced as before. Blacks show no correlation between peer rating and first-grade conduct marks, while whites display consistently positive relationships (significant at the .05 level at midyear). For white children, peer designations of high social standing correspond to teachers' conceptions of good conduct. White children are either responding to the teachers' conduct marks, to some of the same behaviors teachers consider in assigning conduct marks, or to the normative pattern mentioned above.

In sum, partialling out IQ makes black children and white children appear more similar in terms of academic mark-peer-rating correlations, but less similar in terms of conduct mark-peer-rating correlations.

Table 5.9

Correlations between Peer Rating and Grade 1 Marks Controlling IQ (PMA) with the Corresponding Zero-Order Correlations, Working-Class School (Listwise Deletion of Cases for all Correlations)

		Black			White			Combined	
	N	Partial r	Zero-Order r	N	Partial r	Zero-Order r	N	Partial r	Zero-Order r
Child's Mark--Midyear									
Reading	40	0.289	0.454**	18	0.488*	0.469*	58	0.416**	0.461**
Arithmetic	61	0.351**	0.484**	34	0.430*	0.388*	95	0.399**	0.441**
Conduct	61	-0.050	-0.003	34	0.427*	0.409*	95	0.075	0.111
Child's Mark--Year-End									
Reading	63	0.342**	0.466**	34	0.269	0.238	97	0.334**	0.387**
Arithmetic	63	0.367**	0.478**	34	0.359*	0.323	97	0.372**	0.420**
Conduct	63	0.007	-0.006	34	0.335	0.274	97	0.045	0.084

* = significant at p < .05.

** = significant at p < .01.

Absences and Lateness

School records gave the total number of days each child was absent and late in first grade. The average number of absences for first graders in the working-class school, 20.8 days, is noticeably higher than that reported (in chapter 4) for the middle-class school, where, for first graders, the mean number of absences was 8.8 and, for second graders, 7.6. The first-grade difference is significant both in statistical ($p < .01$) and practical terms. One can also note the interaction between sex and race—black girls are absent about as much as black or white boys but white girls are absent more often (table 5.10).

All the correlations between absences and first-grade reading and arithmetic marks presented in table 5.10 are highly significant. A high number of absences corresponds to low substantive area marks. There is a smaller but still significant correlation between absences and children's initial expectations for arithmetic. Otherwise no relations appear between absences and children's expectations.

The most surprising data are the highly significant correlations ($p < .01$) between absences and parents' expectations in both reading and arithmetic. Parents' expectations were obtained before Thanksgiving, for the most part, whereas absences accrue over the entire school year. In the working-class school, parents who had low expectations apparently tended to keep (or allow) their children out of school more. Perhaps these parents feel their children are not likely to profit much from instruction, and, therefore, that missing a day now and then is not a serious loss. This interpretation is supported by the fact that parents' conduct expectations do not correlate significantly with absenteeism. In that conduct is not "taught" in the same sense as reading and arithmetic are, holding high conduct expectations need not instill in a parent any particular incentive for the regular school attendance of his child.

Lateness data are also given in table 5.10. Latenesses are "counted" in this school only when the child is 15 or more minutes late, so the average number of "lates," 11.9, would increase substantially if a more rigid standard were applied. The correlations between lateness and marks are similar to those observed between absences and marks, despite the modest correlation between absences and lateness ($r = 0.246$, $p < .01$). A large number of latenesses is significantly ($p < .01$) associated with poorer marks in reading and arithmetic throughout first grade. Lateness bears no relationship to children's expectations at any time in first grade. The fact that a large number of latenesses is associated significantly ($p < .01$) with poor midyear marks in conduct may indicate that teachers view tardiness as part of children's conduct. The association drops by the end of first grade, however.

Table 5.10

Means and Standard Deviations of Absences and Latenesses
by Race and Sex
Working-Class School, First Grade

	Absences			Latenesses		
	N	Mean	S.D.	N	Mean	S.D.
White Boys	23	19.4	16.8	.	.	
Black Boys	40	18.0	16.2	.	.	
White Girls	28	27.2	19.0	.	.	
Black Girls	38	19.8	13.1	.	.	
Total	129	20.8	16.3	129	11.9	16.8

Correlations of Absences and Latenesses with Other Measures
Working-Class School, First Grade

	Absences		Latenesses	
	N	r	N	r
Parent's Expectation--Midyear				
Reading	105	0.315**	105	0.180
Arithmetic	106	0.287**	106	0.123
Conduct	106	0.076	106	0.059
Child's Expectation--Midyear				
Reading	105	-0.022	105	-0.019
Arithmetic	105	0.211*	105	0.054
Conduct	105	-0.064	105	-0.114
Child's Expectation--Year-End				
Reading	115	-0.020	115	0.077
Artihmetic	116	0.061	116	0.039
Conduct	116	0.046	116	0.094
Child's Mark--Midyear				
Reading	70	0.457**	70	0.384**
Arithmetic	122	0.329**	122	0.326**
Conduct	122	0.140	122	0.252**
Child's Mark--Year-End				
Reading	126	0.377**	126	0.262**
Arithmetic	126	0.283**	126	0.237**
Conduct	126	0.153	126	0.157

* = significant at the .05 level.
** = significant at the .01 level.

The lack of significant correlations between parental expectations and lateness may reflect the greater control children exhibit in this regard (compared to absences), or it may reflect the greater inability of parents to insure prompt attendance. That is, parents expressing both high and low expectations may be about equally prone to the everyday situational contingencies that produce substantial (15 minutes or more) lateness.

The comparable size of the correlations between absences and marks and between lateness and marks argues against "missed time from school" being the sole reason that impaired performance corresponds to a large number of lates.

Standardized Achievement

The working-class school, unlike the middle-class school, did not give standardized achievement tests (such as the Iowa Tests of Basic Skills) to the cohort described in this chapter, even in third grade. The lack is regrettable. In an effort to compensate for this lack, the actual "reader level" teachers reported for each student at the end of second grade was obtained and converted into a grade-level-equivalent score.* The grade-level-equivalent score signifies the level at which a child was actually performing; thus 2.8 would indicate performance at the level of an average ability child who was nearing the end of second grade. As table 5.11 shows, the average achievement for these children at the end of second grade is roughly equivalent to norms for the beginning of second grade.

The measure of standardized reading achievement correlated well with teachers' marks (table 5.11) starting right from the time of the first report card ($r = -0.710$ at midyear and $r = -0.749$ at year-end). The low correlation between IQ (measured in first grade) and standardized reading achievement ($r = 0.071$) (measured at the end of second grade) was unanticipated, particularly since the correlation between IQ and first-grade reading marks (table 5.2) is above .40 and the correlation between marks and achievement is consistently above .70.

What appears to be happening is this: The correlation noted between IQ and reading marks declined substantially in second grade. At the end of second grade the correlation was -0.255, significant at the .05 level, but small in magnitude. There is thus a weak relation between IQ and second-

*We have, up to now through this chapter, been discussing only first-grade data for cohort L-1, but in order to get some standardized achievement bench mark to which marks can be related, we ascertained the reading level attained by these children *after* first grade, at the end of second grade. This kind of de facto performance measure could be superior to measurement based on a short standardized test.

Table 5.11

Correlation of Children's Second-Grade Standardized Reading Achievement
with Other Measures in First Grade, Working-Class School

	N	Mean	S.D.
Standardized Achievement	89	2.152	0.920

	N	r
IQ--PMA in First Grade	70	0.071
Sex (1 = Male, 2 = Female)	89	0.254*
Child's Peer Rating, T2	56	-0.324*
Parent's Reading Expectation, T1	60	-0.340**
Child's Reading Expectation, T1	62	0.172
Child's Reading Expectation, T2	68	0.135
Child's Reading Mark, T1	45	-0.710**
Child's Reading Mark, T2	70	-0.749**

* = significant at p < .05 level.
** = significant at p < .01 level.

grade performance, whether measured in terms of teachers' marks or in terms of a standardized reader, while a strong relation between the two performance measures remains. The decline in the correlation between IQ and standardized reading achievement may be partially due to the decline in the predictive capabilities of IQ tests taken in first grade and also partially due to the slight restriction on the range of the IQ scores for the subsample of cases ($N = 70$) for which data on both IQ and standardized achievement were available.

In line with what was found for middle-class children, there are no significant correlations between these children's first-grade expectations and standardized achievement in reading. There are also essentially zero correlations between these children's expectations and their marks in reading with IQ controlled, a finding that agrees with data for the middle-class school at midyear, but disagrees with what is observed at year-end ($r = 0.237$, $p < .01$, $N = 168$).

Summary

The major finding for working-class children is that there is a general lack of differences associated with race and weaker (or absent) patterns of causal efficacy in the mark-expectation discrepance measures. As noted earlier, both the size of the sample and smaller expectation variances make the power of tests low.

Average expectation levels remained very high for working-class children throughout the year, but individual working-class children did not display the significant above-chance agreement between their expectations early and late in the first-grade year that was noted for middle-class children. The significant negative association between midyear expectations in reading and arithmetic is repeated, however.

Parents in this school had expectations that did not conform well with first marks, even though their expectations were more modest than those of middle-class parents. As in the middle-class school, white parents' expectations are related to IQ but black parents' expectations showed no significant relations to IQ. Unlike the middle-class school, the discrepance between parents' expectations and first marks exerted a small effect on year-end marks. Only the effect for reading barely reached significance.

The major findings can best be presented again in visual diagrams (See figures 5.1, 5.2, 5.3). The diagrams refer to reading, arithmetic, and conduct, respectively, for children of both races combined. Differences between races pointed out earlier will not be mentioned again here. An outstanding characteristic of every diagram is the lack of a path from the child's first expectations to his later expectations.

The discrepance between the child's first expectations and first reading mark does not influence either the child's expectation or his reading mark at year-end. Remarkably little influence on year-end reading marks can be attributed to working-class children's expectations or to feedback stemming from either the parents' or the children's expectation-mark discrepance. Most of the predictors of year-end reading marks—IQ, peer rating, absence, lateness, and previous marks—do not directly involve expectations. For arithmetic, the child's midyear discrepance does affect the year-end mark but the parent discrepance does not. Again, most of the determinants of working-class children's year-end marks do not involve expectations.

The only visual model showing any prediction of working-class children's year-end expectations is that for conduct. The child's midyear mark-expectation discrepance for conduct predicts both later expectations and later marks. The model for conduct differs from the substantive area

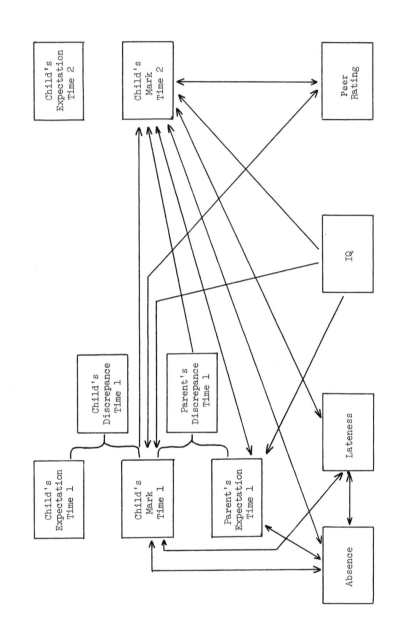

Figure 5.1
Reading Model, Working-Class School, First Grade

Figure 5.2
Arithmetic Model, Working-Class School, First Grade

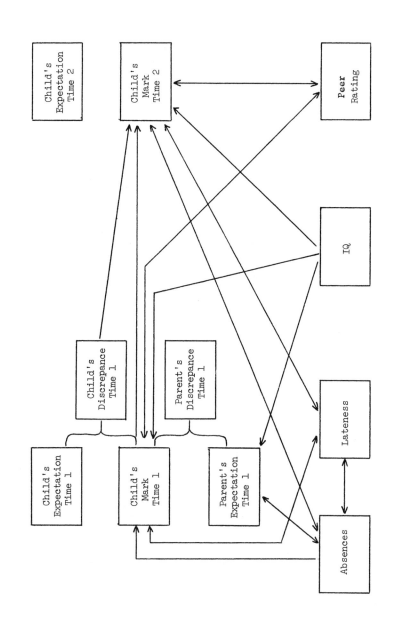

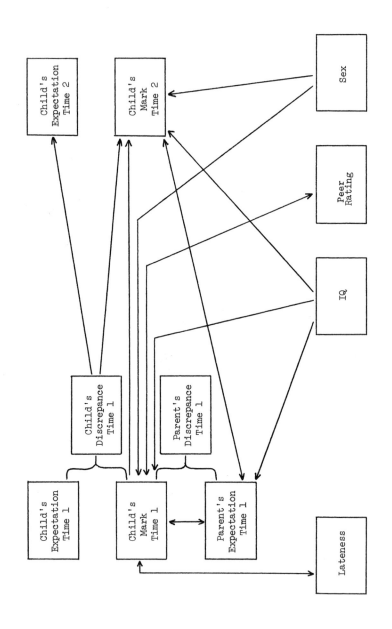

Figure 5.3
Conduct Model, Working-Class School, First Grade

models in several other ways. Not unexpectedly, the child's sex is involved in determining conduct marks; absences are not a predictor in this model. It is somewhat surprising that peer ratings failed to predict year-end conduct marks but did predict both reading and arithmetic marks. Conduct is the only area in which parents are able to predict their child's mark throughout first grade, and this, too, is reflected in the model. The fairly prominent role of IQ in determining conduct marks is surprising, as is the failure of the parents' midyear discrepance to affect conduct marks.

With just this preliminary data, results cannot be pressed too far, but the outstanding pattern seen for working-class children is the impact of ascriptive characteristics like sex and the effects of absence, lateness, and IQ. A second major impression is the refractoriness of these children's expectations. Relatively few relationships involving children's expectations appeared. Third, this research conceptualized interpersonal variables as important for early school performance, but such interpersonal variables (especially parent's expectations) do not appear very influential regarding first-grade performance of working-class children in reading and arithmetic. The most substantial difference between the working-class children of this school and the middle-class children of the other school is the differential scholastic attainment of the two groups on standardized measures of reading in later grades despite the similarity in talent and the similarity in the quality of academic programs available.

CHAPTER 6

An Overview of the Findings across Schools

It is now time to place the major findings of chapters 3, 4, and 5 in context with each other. Before doing this we remind the reader that the research described in this book consists of two extensive case studies—studies of two schools. How far the findings apply in other schools is difficult to ascertain. Determining to what extent case study results may be generalized is very much a matter of judgment, and depends on the number and representativeness of the "cases." This research sacrificed broad coverage for a detailed understanding of causal mechanisms at work in children's earliest experiences in two schools. To aid the reader in determining how typical or atypical the two schools were, we provided 1970 census data for the communities served by the schools (table 2.1) and some data from a recent Maryland accountability survey (appendix A to chapter 2). It is our impression that the schools are fairly typical of middle- and working-class schools.

Chapters 3, 4, and 5 show that working-class and middle-class children in the two schools do differ by some major parameters of the study design. The data reveal, for example, that the expectations middle-class children held were lower and more veridical than those of working-class children. We would like to know exactly why such a difference appears; we want to know what school activities, what attitudes or expectancies of parents, what kinds of treatment by teachers, and what other influences have led to this difference. We want to know not only how middle-class and working-class first graders differ but, if possible, the causal explanations for the differences.

Providing unequivocal causal explanations is difficult because several variables are completely confounded in this research. Social class in particular is confounded with school-related variables—such things as school marking policies, IQ differences, and racial or integration effects. This study was observational, so, in general, it cannot separate out the analytically independent effects of these factors, although in some instances the particular nature of the results does allow an "unpackaging" of the confounded variables. One important instance of this occurs when the middle-class and working-class schools as a whole differ in some way, yet where the results for the white subsample of the working-class school resemble results for the all-white middle-class school. In such instances inter-school differences cannot be a simple social-class effect, since whites in the two schools came from different class backgrounds. Such effects must be attributed to race or some variable associated with race.

In beginning the review we reiterate several ways the two schools differ or are the same with respect to racial composition, socioeconomic status, IQ level, marking policies, and staff quality.

The middle-class school is all white, while the working-class school enrolls about 60% black students. In addition, about 50% of the staff in the working-class school is black, while at the time of this study no staff of the middle-class school was black.

The average family income in the middle-class area is roughly twice what it is in the working-class area. A pronounced difference in socioeconomic status like that existing between these two schools usually signals an equally pronounced difference in IQ-test performance. The observed difference in average IQ between schools is statistically significant, but not large. First graders in cohorts S-1 and L-1 had average IQ's of 115 vs. 103, respectively, but this inter-school difference turned out to be not much larger than the difference for one cohort as it moved from one year to the next within the same school (S-1 at first and second grades). The average IQ for cohort S-1 on the Short Form of the Stanford Test of Mental Maturity in second grade was 104, compared to 115 on the PMA for the same children in first grade. Differences in average IQ between schools, therefore, were not much larger than year-to-year differences in the same cohort. This bench mark, although certainly useful, cannot specify a complete lack of IQ effects, given the complexities of sampling variability, test differences, age effects, and the like, but it indicates that IQ is potentially confounded to a much smaller extent than one might have originally expected. The selection of these two schools for research was fortunate in this respect.

The range of IQ's of working-class children commonly exceeds the range for middle-class children (see, for example, Wilson, 1963:200), so the observed standard deviations of 11.0 for the middle-class school and 13.7 for the working-class school are in the expected direction. But, since the variability of IQ within the schools is also more similar than expected, the correlations within the two schools between IQ and other variables ought to be similarly affected, or unaffected, by the range of IQ scores. Differences in strengths of IQ associations between the two schools, then, are not obvious statistical artifacts.

Another systematic difference between schools is marking policies. In the working-class school, as has already been noted in several places, each child's performance is supposedly evaluated in relation to the performance considered average for his grade level, while in the middle-class school marks are supposed to indicate the child's effort independent of actual ability. Actual implementation of these policies differed from one year to the next. The effect of marking policies on school differences is far from clear-cut, nevertheless, possible effects of marking policies receive considerable attention in what follows.

The size and quality of staff in the two schools, fortunately, were very similar. The staff of the working-class school had slightly better credentials and was assisted by more supplemental resource teachers. The rather large difference in second-grade reading achievement between the two schools, therefore, cannot be written off as a consequence of a lack of school resources.

Naturally we need not be concerned with inter-school differences when reporting similar findings for both schools, and the more the schools differ in such cases the more certain we can be that the differentiating dimensions are not implicated in the production of any effects.

Children's Expectations

The areas of reading and arithmetic were picked for study because they form the heart of the elementary-school curriculum. Conduct was studied because it is academically vacuous and, so, in a sense, serves to capture halo effects and other nonacademic variations. Williams (1976) has pointed recently to "affective" as compared with "cognitive" evaluations by teachers; something of the same distinction can be drawn here, when teachers' ratings of reading and arithmetic are compared to their ratings of conduct. Reading and arithmetic expectations also make a nice contrast because of their potential linkage to one another and to sex roles.

All first-grade children, whether middle- or working-class, failed to predict their first report card marks in reading, arithmetic, or conduct with any accuracy. Some children, of course, were correct, but their numbers were no greater than chance would predict. Children in neither school, apparently, had much idea what marks they would get in any subject when they started school. All held expectations that were too high. The expectations of working-class children, furthermore, were inordinately high.

VALIDITY AND RELIABILITY

A natural first question is whether children's initial overestimation should be taken at face value. Perhaps the children did not understand what they were doing when they were asked about expectations. Perhaps the children overestimated their forthcoming marks because they were ashamed to acknowledge to the interviewers anything less than high expectations.

There is no absolute response to such speculations. On the other hand, we were acutely aware of possible threats to validity and took several steps to improve validity and/or check it. First, every interviewing session in which expectations were obtained was conducted in private and in the spirit of a game. Interviewers tried hard to get children to ''guess'' without pressing them. Also, as stated in chapter 2, it is doubtful if the children were even aware their ''guesses'' were being recorded. Second, real efforts were made to insure that every child knew what was being asked. At the time of the initial interviews, when children guessed what they would get on their first report card, they were gently asked at the beginning of the interview if they knew the meaning of ''report card,'' ''arithmetic,'' and so on. A large plastic replica of a report card helped define the task. This brightly colored plastic sheet was spread out on a table or on the floor. Interviewers took as much time with each child as was needed, and only after the interviewer was satisfied the child understood what was being asked did the interview proceed. In short, the procedures used for gathering data were designed with an eye to enhancing the validity of the measures, as well as to safeguarding the dignity of the child. (In this connection we might add that we have carried out considerable research with other children in these schools on other topics and, in fact, became so familiar to persons in the schools that many assumed we were regular school employees.)

Later in the school year validity of the expectation measure was checked by reinterviewing every first grader in cohort S-2 of the middle-class school and every first grader in cohort L-1 of the working-class school. The purpose was to see whether children's understanding of report cards and of the marking system was clear enough for them to have been expected to make a meaningful response in the ''expectation interview'' held earlier. At this later time interviewers did not ask children to report expectations but, instead, probed the children's understanding of report cards by asking questions such as: ''What are report cards?'' ''What do reading and arithmetic mean?'' ''What do the numbers 1, 2, 3, and 4 on the report card mean?'' This probing interview was undertaken by an interviewer different from the one who had done the earlier expectation interviews, and the probe was designed to check, independently, on the children's comprehension of what had been asked earlier in the year.

All children at the time of the reinterview (late in first grade) seemed to know the major fact about report cards—that report cards evaluate how well children do in school. In the middle-class school about 90% of children, and in the working-class school about 70% of children had a very good grasp of the report cards, according to the second interviewer's ratings. "Very good grasp" means a full understanding of the nature and meaning of report cards, an unequivocal understanding of the subject areas being marked, and a clear notion of the marking system, as well as, of course, the willingness to verbalize all this. That a smaller percentage of working-class first graders had a "very good grasp" may reflect, in part, the confusing system used to give marks in reading in their school. It may also reflect the commonly found reluctance of working-class children to talk with adults as easily as middle-class children do. The children in the working-class school had received more report cards than the middle-class children by the end of first grade because they received report cards in kindergarten. Their understanding of report cards was based on two years' experience, and therefore may have exceeded what the probing interview was able to gauge.

Most of this discussion of validity could be termed "subjective evidence." The best objective evidence for the validity of the expectation measure consists of the meaningful and consistent relationships that emerged between it and other variables. More is said of this later.

As for reliability, using a single question to determine expectations in each area (namely, reading, arithmetic, and conduct) definitely limits evidence bearing on reliability. In one classroom, however, a test-retest reliability check was reassuring. In this classroom the expectation sampling procedure was carried out on two occasions one week apart, and a high degree of concordance ($r = 0.76$) was found between expectations elicited on the two occasions. (Since test-retest procedures pose obvious threats to a longitudinal research plan, use of such procedures was limited.) Persistence of expectations over first grade can also be regarded as a test-retest measure, of course, but, because of the long intervening time interval, we prefer to regard agreement between expectations at the middle and end of first grade as a substantive finding.

SOCIAL CLASS DIFFERENCES

We were surprised that initial expectations of working-class children for both reading and conduct were higher than those of middle-class children. We were even more surprised that working-class children's expectations for reading and for conduct remained above those of middle-class children at the end of first grade. Unreliability is not a likely explanation for the difference between schools, because, although unreliability could lead to attenuation of correlations between expectations and other factors, it alone should not lead to large biases in the mean.

Several things might lead one to expect lower forecasts of marks by working-class children than by middle-class children, the opposite of what we found. Working-class children's expectations might be expected to be more modest because their older siblings and friends probably did less well in school than the older siblings and friends of middle-class children did. Working-class parents held lower expectations, on the average, than middle-class parents did, so the level of parents' views might have produced the difference. The greater social distance between teachers and children in the working-class school might also be thought to depress children's expectations. (Class differences between teachers and pupils are often cited as a cause of low teacher expectations.) Despite all the reasons just cited and, no doubt, others that would account for one predicting that working-class children's expectations would be lower, the opposite was observed—and observed consistently within both racial groups.

The counter-intuitive finding of high expectations for lower-class first graders is not out of line with empirical findings for older children, however. College aspirations of black adolescents, for example, are often found to be out of line both with their likelihood of attending college and with the realistic steps they have taken toward fulfilling such aspirations.

But it is the mismatch between working-class children's expectations and their teachers' evaluation of their performance rather than the absolute level of their expectations that deserves emphasis. Some of these children, their teachers tell us, start school expecting to learn to read on the first day. Even in arithmetic, where there was almost no difference between schools in children's expectations, the much poorer performance of the working-class children led to mismatch.

Lack of a difference in arithmetic expectations by social class or race is interesting. When combined with the observation that children's expectations for arithmetic were lower than their expectations for other subjects in both schools, it suggests the anxiety "numbers" arouse in children is pervasive. It is also further evidence of validity. Lack of a difference in arithmetic expectations by social class combined with the presence of a difference in reading and conduct expectations suggests that children consistently differentiate among areas of expectations between schools as well as within schools.

Working-class parents expressed much lower expectations for both reading and arithmetic than middle-class parents did. Both sets of parents, however, expected about the same performance in conduct. Patterns of parental and children's expectations, then, did not closely coincide in either school, but in the working-class school, where parental expectations were relatively lower and children's expectations were relatively higher, lack of agreement between expectations of parents and children was more striking. The only persons who predicted first marks in reading with measurable accuracy were middle-class parents.

The level of middle-class children's expectations was generally higher than the first marks awarded, but both the difference between children's expectations and their marks and between children's expectations and parents' expectations were much smaller in the middle-class school than in the working-class school. Middle-class children tend to have "too great expectations," but working-class children have astonishingly "too great expectations." Middle-class parents are the only persons "well-tuned" in this respect.

One consequence of the very high level of working-class children's expectations is that the variability of their expectations is small—smaller than either the variability of their marks or of their parents' expectations. The variability of children's initial expectations in the middle-class school, on the other hand, is not only larger than that of working-class children's, but larger than the variability of their parents' expectations and of the marks they received. Their estimates encompass a wide range. The inaccuracies, then, of children in the two schools are of a very different sort qualitatively.

In chapter 5 we repeatedly pointed to the restriction on the range of working-class children's expectations as a likely explanation for why relationships between expectations and other variables did not emerge or were attenuated. It is well known that restricted variance attenuates the reliability of a measure, and both this attenuation and the restricted range per se could lead correlations with other variables to be small. It is also a fact, of course, that inordinately high expectations could be an especially cogent cause of poor performance, even though we could not show this without observing children with more veridical expectations in a similar environment. Since so few children had low expectations we could not analyze meaningfully how performance varied by expectation level.

DIFFERENCES BY SUBJECT MATTER

In our opinion some of the most cogent evidence for the validity of the expectation measure is that in both schools children clearly differentiated between their expectations for reading and arithmetic. Children expect to do better, on the average, in reading than in arithmetic, and there is a significant undermatching between children's initial expectations for these two subjects in both schools. If the high level and restricted range of children's expectations in the working-class school meant that expectations were not being measured *at all* in this school, replication of the "negative" relation between expectations in reading and arithmetic in the working-class school would be very unlikely. Only 25% of the children in the middle-class school have the same initial expectations in reading and arithmetic, and only 28% have the same expectations in the working-class school. These percentages are close enough to suggest that children behave in a similar way in the two locales with respect to the two subject areas. At the end of the year the deficit of matching between reading and arithmetic expectations is still present, but the deficit is not large enough to be significant in either school. Again, the pattern of behavior across both schools is similar.

The inverse association in children's expectations for reading and arithmetic contrasts sharply with parents' expectations in both schools, and also contrasts with the positive correlation between marks actually given by teachers in reading and arithmetic in both schools. Since matching between children's expectations in the two areas increased over the year, the teachers' behavior and parents' expectations may exert some pull to make those expectations more consistent.

Children's differentiation of expectations by area, in addition to being a strong point of consistency between schools, agrees with what has been found for older children (see Crandall, 1969, and Morse, 1967). If children were merely giving high guesses because they thought this was what the interviewer wanted to hear or because they did not understand what they were doing, one would not expect undermatching. No matching or, possibly, overmatching would be more likely.

The undermatching between arithmetic and reading in the working-class school is particularly impressive and important, because there the highly skewed expectation distributions and the failure of expectations and marks in reading to move significantly toward consistency over first grade provided less information on validity from other sources than was available in the middle-class school. Naturally the relatively weak movement toward consistency in arithmetic and conduct is evidence of validity of the expectation construct, but the consistent and unequivocal undermatching of reading and arithmetic, which agrees with other research and with the similar counterintuitive finding in the middle-class school, strikes us as the most persuasive evidence for the construct validity of the expectations measure in the working-class school.

Undermatching between children's expectations in reading and arithmetic (high expectations for reading are apt to be paired with not-so-high expectations for arithmetic) probably reflect norms present in both social classes. Most Americans make light of poor performance in arithmetic—the "I-can't-balance-a-checkbook" phenomenon—but we have yet to see a parent who does not take poor performance in reading seriously. One often hears adults jokingly comment on their inability to "add two and two." These same persons, however, would not take lightly either their own or their children's illiteracy. As a consequence, children may experience less pressure for high aspirations in arithmetic.

The undermatching of reading and arithmetic expectations has practical and policy implications of some importance. First, if children's expectations are distinct in different subjects at the time children start school, low expectations in one subject need not affect learning in another. Second, if changing children's expectations proved, in the future, to be either feasible or desirable, the likelihood of bringing about useful change by some "treatment" appears to us to be greater, given that the target of change could be restricted; that is, one can more easily imagine a set of exercises to improve a child's ideas about his ability in arithmetic than one can imagine a set of exercises to improve a child's entire self-image.

LACK OF RACIAL DIFFERENCES

We saw that expectations of black children and white children in the working-class school did not differ substantially (with the single exception that white children were somewhat less optimistic about arithmetic than black children at the time of the first report card). Since minority-group members are often presumed to have low expectations for themselves, that is, they are assumed to regard themselves in the same poor light as the majority of society regards them, the reader may find the parity between racial groups perplexing. The assumption that black children have negative self-images, although intuitively plausible, has not survived empirical test, however. An avalanche of recent self-concept studies shows that blacks do not necessarily have lower self-concepts than whites. High self-esteem for black and other minority-group children is seen as a consequence of the youngsters' living in protective contexts (Rosenberg and Simmons, 1971). There the children do not have access to information concerning their relative status in the larger society. If a child from a broken home has many classmates also from broken homes, the stigma of a broken home is greatly reduced, for example.

In the particular working-class school of this study the social context seems especially protective, despite the school's mixed racial populations. This school has been integrated for a number of years, so the whole issue of race is deemphasized. In other work (unpublished) with older children in this same school, we found, for example, that fifth graders had equal numbers of same-race and opposite-race friends in school, and that rates of volunteering in small-group experiments were the same for black as for white children. Also, when asked whether they would prefer a white teacher or black teacher "next year," neither white children nor black children in this school expressed any preference. Perhaps most revealing of all was the observation that fifth graders in a social studies class in this school were surprised to learn that blacks were a minority group in America!

Whatever the cause, the equivalence of expectations we observed for blacks and whites in first grade is contrary to what others have found for older children and for mixed groups. Cohen (1972) noted with junior-high-school children that only when black children were given extensive prior coaching at a task (such as constructing a crystal set) and the superior performance of blacks was documented on videotape did white workmates accord equal status to blacks in work groups.

Equality of expectations is consistent, however, with results from some experiments carried out with older children to raise their expectations (see Entwisle and Webster, 1974b). It was just as easy to raise expectations of black children as those of white children. Cohen may have been observing an "unnatural" depression of black children's expectations because the black children were brought into strange new situations with white children whom they had never seen before. Blacks may then voice low expectations for themselves because, by that age, they have learned that whites generally hold low expectations for blacks in unfamiliar situations. Also, universities and scientists may be more unfamiliar and, therefore, more threatening to blacks than to whites undergoing laboratory experiments. Children who participated in our field experiments, as well as those in the present research, worked together on a daily basis in mixed-race classrooms, so the social context of the research matched the children's ordinary social context.

How Children's Expectations Change over Time

Children's expectations generally exceeded marks at midyear in both schools. One would think, therefore, that expectations would decrease over the first-grade year. Quite the opposite happened. Average expectation levels were *higher* at the end of first grade than at midyear in the middle-class school. In the working-class school initial expectations exceeded marks by a huge margin, yet expectations stayed at about the same level in reading and in arithmetic over the year and declined only moderately in conduct. As we have already discussed, there was no substantial difference in the way expectations of blacks and whites changed over the first-grade year.

Middle-class children did get better at anticipating their marks over the first-grade year. At midyear their marks and expectations did not match significantly in any area. Their year-end marks and expectations in reading did agree significantly, however, and agreement approached significance at the end of the year for both arithmetic and conduct. Agreement increased because middle-class children became better at *not* underestimating what to expect in reading and conduct. Substantial numbers of children underestimated the marks they would receive on the first report card, but children presumably learned quickly that teachers gave almost no one the lowest mark (D) and gave only a few C's. Middle-class children were much less likely to revise their hopes in a downward than in an upward direction. Most of the increase in agreement for middle-class children came from upward revision of expectations. (The apparent reduction of overestimation for arithmetic came about because marking standards became more lenient as the year went on—children's expectations actually increased over the year.) When middle-class children's expectations and marks disagreed, the majority still had expectations too high in reading and conduct, but not in arithmetic.

Working-class children, on the other hand, did not have expectations that significantly matched marks in *any* of the three areas at midyear or at year-end. Their high expectations—much higher than middle-class children's—were not modified over the year despite the low marks given by their teachers. In chapter 5 we gave some possible reasons for the failure of low midyear marks to modify high expectations. Among these reasons was the paradox of strong face-to-face reinforcement in the classroom coupled with severe marking on report cards. There is more discussion of this in a later section.

EXPECTATIONS OVER SECOND GRADE

Middle-class children's expectations declined between the end of first grade and the middle of second grade and then, over second grade, increased slightly, rising to a level equal to that observed at the beginning of first grade. Children's expectations for reading were, again, consistently the highest of those for any area, but differences among the areas were tiny. At midyear second grade, children's expectations and marks still did not match to a significant degree for either reading or arithmetic, but there was highly significant matching in all three areas by the end of the year. Close to 60% of children correctly anticipated their marks in reading and arithmetic at the end of second grade. (At the end of first grade 55% of the children correctly predicted their reading mark, while 48% correctly predicted their arithmetic mark.) Middle-class children, then, made steady progress over their first two school years toward accurate prediction, but their accuracy was not great enough to be significant in all three areas until the end of second grade.

The gradual improvement in agreement over the first two grades and the significant agreement observed by the end of second grade is decisive evidence in favor of studying children early in their school careers. It is plausible to see a feedback process between marks and expectations leading to large adjustments in the first few cycles—the noticeable modulation of the lowest expectations, for example, as middle-class children become familiar with social reality. Then, as time passes, the process damps down.

We studied first and second graders because pilot work and other evidence (like Rist's 1970 report) convinced us that expectations might be most important in a child's early encounters with the social system of the school. If research were delayed until fourth grade (when children can be queried by written instruments) all the decisive feedback might already have occurred. In the same vein, the impact of different influences on expectations may vary early in the process of expectation building. Middle-class parents' expectations, for example, in our data, are rather more important in first grade than in second. It is almost as if parents' causal potential were being stockpiled over the first five or six years of a child's life and then released during the first grade. After that the parent begins to recede into the background and exerts less and less force on school performance. Such a model seems sensible, and is consistent with the notion that parents initially constitute an independent force in the overall system while later their reliance on their child's mark history in the formation of their expectations decreases their unique influence.

Marks

With all the attention that has been given over the last decade to resources of school systems, both matériel and personnel, it is hard to understand why the actual marks teachers give have been almost ignored. This gap in research is particularly striking in light of a recent statement by Dornbusch and Scott (1975). They point out that a rational model is useful in studying control systems, not because such a model is necessarily true, but because such a model serves as a means of detecting problems in existing control systems. Some first-grade classrooms studied in this research, it turns out, exemplify all four of the ways Dornbusch and Scott enumerate for low performance evaluations to occur through no fault of the performer.

One way is for the participant to receive contradictory evaluations. Another way is for participants to be evaluated for performances over

which they lack control. A third way involves performers being unable to
predict the relation between the work performed and its evaluation. The
fourth way occurs when performers are expected to meet unattainable
standards.

These four problems, from our perspective at least, are much more
likely to occur in the working-class than in the middle-class school. For the
working-class school we have already noted the stark contrast between the
positive informal feedback of the Distar reading program and the negative
formal feedback of report cards (problem one) and the marking policy
based on ability, an unresponsive dimension, rather than on effort, a more
controllable dimension (problem two). Working-class first graders are unable to predict the relation between their work and its evaluation—our data
show no congruence between their expectations and their marks in first
grade (problem three). In addition, standards are "unattainable" for most
children because about 40% received D's on their first report card while a
large majority of them expected A's (problem four). Both the marking
policy and the higher level of marks make the four problems much less
likely in the middle-class school.

Differences between average first marks in the two schools were
enormous. In reading the average first mark was 1.77 (a little over a B) in
the middle-class school. It was 3.15 (between a D and a C) in the
working-class school. Even at the end of first grade the average reading
mark in the working-class school was almost a full unit below that in the
middle-class school (2.59 vs. 1.73). Most working-class children got D's
and C's in first grade, whereas middle-class children got A's and B's.

The disparity in children's performance is perplexing, given the
above-average IQ levels of both schools and the relatively small difference
between schools in average IQ. Marking policies in the two schools may
play a role, but the role is not simple. For one thing, the stated policies in
their "ideal" forms differ from the policies implemented in both places. In
neither school is the policy rigidly adhered to over an extensive time
period. The patterns of relationships between IQ and marks (strong relations for working-class first graders and weak or absent relationships for
middle-class first graders) underscore how divergent the marking policies
in the two schools were early in first grade. Correlations between IQ and
marks were considerably larger in second grade than in first grade in the
middle-class school, however, so effort could not have been the only
criterion used in marking in second grade. Ability gained in importance. It
seems middle-class teachers strayed from "official policy" as they faced
the day-to-day needs of teaching in second grade.

Some data for the working-class school beyond the period of this
research suggest IQ-mark correlations in second grade there declined to a

point where the correlations became almost comparable in the two schools, despite the opposite marking policies. This is just what would be predicted if marks were beginning to be based on factors other than sheer ability in the working-class school. There the policy of marking children solely in terms of grade-level norms was apparently not a policy teachers could adhere to for more than one year, probably because the children found the specified goals almost impossible to attain.

The increasing influence of IQ in the middle-class school could come about as follows. Parental expectations and IQ are substantially correlated and the parental mark-expectation discrepance was effective in producing mark changes, so the increase in the importance of IQ could stem from the indirect effect of IQ on marks via parental expectations. That is, the causal efficacy of parental expectations in the middle-class school is likely to bring about changes in children's marks that increase the observed correlation between IQ and marks because parental expectations are initially correlated with IQ. In the working-class school little or no such indirect supplementary action would be expected because parental expectations in that school exerted little if any effect.

This causal sequence in the middle-class school could also be bolstered by the increasing difficulty teachers must experience in separating ability from effort. As subject matter increases in complexity, sheer effort may have little pay-off; successful performance in reading in second grade, for example, depends heavily on prior success in first grade. As time passes teachers must find it more and more difficult to differentiate effort from ability. "The-child-must-have-been-trying-because-it-was-learned" is a syndrome that would also produce an increasing correlation between IQ and marks.

In the middle-class school, it seems to us, children are being "gentled" into the system—allowed a year to try their wings without negative sanctions being applied. In the working-class school, on the other hand, the first year in school is an abrasive brush with reality. By second grade however, mark-IQ correlations behaved as if "reality" had been redefined. By second grade, we suspect, there was little difference in de facto marking policies between schools.

Teachers in the schools are not likely to be aware of the overall pattern of events we have just described because different teachers are involved with a child at different times. Each teacher gets only a piece of the overall picture and is not privy to information in the form we have assembled it.

Our data shed further light on marking practices and on the actual incentives that children may consequently perceive as being offered them. First of all, case-by-case differences in marking from one year to the next in the middle-class school were amazingly large. There was no significant

matching between the marks given a child at the end of first grade and
those given him in the middle of second grade, even though within each
grade there was considerable consistency in individual children's marks.
What a cloudy picture this must offer six- or seven-year-old children trying
to monitor behavior. Even more surprising is that so many very poor marks
(up to 40%) were given in the working-class school on the first report card.
Clearly this was unanticipated by parents and by children. How such negative and disappointing events affect parents and children, we do not know.
We did not, for example, ask parents or children how they felt about the
marks given on report cards. We do suspect, as already discussed in chapter 5, that when feedback is extremely negative children may insulate
themselves against it. The failure of expectations to fall can be taken as
evidence of failure to process negative feedback. Such insulation has advantages for preserving the self-image, but it has serious disadvantages in
terms of monitoring or evaluating performance. If children shield themselves from knowledge of the quality of their performance, they are not in a
rational position to alter it.

The implications of the two different marking systems in the two
schools and the way in which both marking systems change over time
could have profound effects in terms of the long-range performance of
children. One group of children learns that marks are predictable; the other
group learns that the system is inscrutable to their parents as well as to
them. The results seen here may or may not be representative of how
middle-class and working-class children more generally are inducted into
school, but, irrespective of class, there are many schools that adopt one
policy or the other. Little prior evaluation of these policies, to our knowledge, has previously been attempted.

OTHER COMMENTS ON MARKING PRACTICES

In both schools marks in reading and arithmetic matched significantly
throughout first grade. Teachers see better or poorer performance in both
areas by the same children, in other words. In the middle-class school
conduct marks showed significant matching with both reading and arithmetic marks at all times during the first grade. In the working-class school
there was generally no relationship between conduct and marks in the
academic areas (an exception being arithmetic at year-end).

The congruence of marks in the academic areas is not surprising.
Marks should be related, whether marking is in terms of grade norms or of
effort. Marking in terms of grade norms should produce conduct marks that
are reasonably independent of academic marks, as was observed in the
working-class school. Marking in terms of effort might be expected ini-

tially to produce academic area marks that show a relation to conduct marks, because behavioral manifestations of effort may appear to teachers as similar to children's general attempts to "behave well." The observed relationship between marks in conduct and the substantive areas suggested that just such a halo effect was present in middle-class teachers' marking.

In both schools, marks in all three areas are significantly consistent in first grade, and about half the children received the same mark at midyear and year-end. Throughout the second year, about two-thirds of the children received identical midyear and year-end marks. In vibrant contrast to the persistence of marks within the first and second grades, marks did not match between the end of first grade and the beginning of second grade, however. This confusion in feedback between years may partially explain why children in cohort S-1 were not able to predict their marks accurately until late in the second grade. Marks in second grade actually were unpredictable from the marks received in first grade.

A few other comments about marking are in order. First, asking teachers to evaluate each child in 22 areas, as the report card required, is a difficult task when a teacher must rate 20 or 30 children. Our pilot work suggested that most first-grade children understood what was being rated in reading, arithmetic, and conduct, but that children did not understand other areas that were rated (such as spelling or language). We tried initially (in 1969 and 1970 pilot studies) to elicit children's expectations for spelling, but the children just did not understand what spelling was. Whether children should be assigned a mark in an area they cannot define is a serious question, especially in light of Dornbusch and Scott's statements. Too many marks may also be dangerous because children may fail to process feedback for important areas and, instead, process feedback for an area that is not important. Children could pay attention to marks in physical education and music and feel they were doing well, for example, even though they had poor marks in reading and arithmetic.

The analysis of marks also shows that marks are far from being distributed over the available range. Depending upon which school is being considered, there is a thrust toward the floor or ceiling of the mark distribution in first-grade marks. In each place the distribution is skewed. Marks are so high in the middle-class school that there is little room for improvement after marks are given at the end of first grade. This skewing makes a readjustment in second grade mandatory, and this may not be welcomed by either the children or the second-grade teacher. If children continue to try as hard in second grade as they did in first, for example, they may be mystified by a mark decline. The second grade teacher, however, may not think it feasible to give 50% of the students A's.

First-grade teachers, by marking so close to the ceiling, could also create a ceiling for achievement. Improvement in marks, as we have seen, occurs when expectations exceed marks. There is not much possibility for such gaps between expectations and marks in the middle-class school, because the marks assigned are so high. Being too close to the ceiling appears preferable to having teachers mark too close to the floor (as in the working-class school), because punishment seems to have much more complex effects than reinforcement, but it might be better in both places to change to a marking scale that has a wider range and to aim for more symmetrical distributions, with room for change in either direction. An expanded scale would reduce the constraints imposed by ceiling effects and, perhaps, enhance the relative importance of mark-expectation discrepancies in determining later marks and expectations. Such a change implies other changes that should be carefully studied—for example, a scale with 7 or 9 points would reduce the degree of *exact* matching between children's marks and expectations, thereby possibly increasing children's anxiety.

The brief investigation of actual marks and how they are assigned that we report in this book leads us to think that far too little attention has been given to *what actually happens* when marks are given out. The giving of a mark is a relatively simple act; its consequences are more complex. The mark affects behavior of several people for a considerable time afterward.

Marks have complex effects, furthermore, because marks themselves are complex. The correlation between conduct marks and academic marks for middle-class children can be taken as evidence that teachers are rating something in addition to academic performance when they assign some marks. We also know that marks are not unidimensional from the less-than-perfect correlations between teachers' marks and scores on standardized achievement tests. Marks are often thought to be a compound of a performance rating and a subjective rating, the latter reflecting teachers' "affective biases."

"Affective bias" is a term meant to cover (1) teachers' expectations that are a consequence of children's characteristics other than actual performance level—dialect, for instance, or being the sibling of a previous high or low performer; (2) the necessities imposed by logistical problems—there has to be a way to signal both improvement and deterioration in performance, so the average mark cannot be too high (or too low) at the beginning of a school year if a teacher is to be able to control reinforcement; and (3) the "special case"—the child who is out sick for a long time may be judged leniently, while a child who is absent for other reasons may be judged strictly.

Sometimes in this book we have viewed marks as "objective performance ratings" and at other times we have emphasized the more arbitrary aspects of marks—the (teachers') subjective element in marks or the selection of school marking policies. We have done this depending upon which aspect was more salient in the context of a particular discussion. Marks are neither totally arbitrary nor totally objective performance measures. We have no index of performance other than teachers' marks in first grade, so we have no choice but to use marks as a dependent variable to measure how expectations affect performance. Yet in successive feedback cycles, say, in predicting how first-grade marks affect second-grade expectations, it seems prudent to emphasize the compound nature of teachers' marks, because the data show that middle-class children at least are becoming aware of the distribution of marks—the average and range of the distribution are both conditioned by teachers' "affective bias" and administrative decisions concerning marking policies.

Discrepances between Marks and Expectations

The main purpose of this research was to uncover causal relations—if they existed—that involved children's expectations and performance. Average expectation levels or simple correlations provide little basis for inferring causal effects. The following sections, therefore, examine change from one semester to the next. The temporal ordering of the observation periods allows us to specify changes that occur subsequent to various antecedent conditions, and therefore assists in specifying causal orderings.

The data are not extensive enough to allow us to propose completely specified causal models, but many of the findings for each school have been summarized in the form of visual models (presented at the ends of chapters 3, 4, and 5). The reader should be warned here, again, that, although the models aid in organizing the data, the elements and relationships included in (or excluded from) them are tentative. The reader should also bear in mind that these visual diagrams by no means exhaust the findings. In fact, some of the most provocative findings, such as the undermatching between children's expectations for reading and arithmetic or the lack of correlation between black parents' expectations for their children and their children's IQ, cannot be portrayed in these diagrams. We tried to include important findings that could be portrayed in two-dimensional diagrams.

In imagining how expectations operate, one might think that children who get high marks are more astute and, therefore, that they would be better at forecasting their marks. We saw this was not the case, however, for when expectation-mark agreement was stratified by mark received at midyear first grade, children of all performance levels and of both social classes seemed to formulate their expectations in the same way before the first report card. Children who received A's and those who received D's showed approximately the same distribution of expectations, as did those in between. This hypothesis was most fully examined with data for the middle-class children, but certainly nothing for them or in the more constrained data for lower-class children contradicts the assertion that both the level and accuracy of children's initial expectations are independent of their ability. The lack of significant correlations between IQ and children's expectations in both schools provides further support for this assertion.

Another reasonable hypothesis is that children with low or moderate expectations, when compared to children with high expectations, would manifest a high amount of agreement between forecasts for their first report card and their actual performance because a poor or average performance is more definitely under the child's control. Middle-class children who forecast low marks (and they were relatively few in number) or moderate marks, however, got about the same percentage of low and moderate marks as the class as a whole. This line of reasoning, apparently, is also incorrect.

For working-class children the combination of exceedingly high children's expectations with relatively low mark assignments severely restricts possible patterns of outcomes, but for the case most amenable to parallel analysis in the working-class school (namely, in arithmetic at year-end), the results appear identical to those seen in the middle-class school—neither children's performance level nor expectation level per se produced effects that influenced the accuracy of children's expectations.

The discrepance between children's marks and expectations, however, apparently does have some predictive power from the time of the first report card on, even though marks or expectations alone are not good predictors of each other at subsequent times. The effects of prior discrepances can be seen clearly in the middle-class school in both grades, and the data available for the working-class school point to the same conclusions.

The majority of children ought to expect the same mark at year-end as was received at midyear—there was actually great consistency in marks awarded. (Generally, more than 60% of the children were awarded identical marks at the two times.) There is, nevertheless, a consistent excess of cases where marks move up, down, or remain stationary in the precise way required to reduce (minimize) an earlier discrepancy between marks and expectations. That is, there was a consistent overrepresentation of the following types of cases: a child's mark remained the same if the mark equalled what he expected; a child's mark went down if he did better than he had expected; and a child's mark went up if he did worse than he had expected. The excess of these types of changes is significant for reading and conduct in first grade and for all three areas in second grade. In both years, over half the middle-class children whose marks improved in reading, arithmetic, or conduct belonged to the group who did not do as well as they expected at midyear. Working-class children whose arithmetic and conduct marks improved over first grade were also disproportionately recruited from among children who earlier expected to do better than they actually did.

The changes in marks as a consequence of a prior discrepance are, thus, of several types, and the changes are seen in both schools. The consistency of these patterns is impressive both because of the complexity of these data and because of the unreliability that characterizes all measures of such young children. We are persuaded that these results document a causal role for expectations in a natural setting.

This discussion has been oriented to "marks" or "performance" as a dependent variable. How does feedback affect expectations as a dependent variable? As expectations are modified, they, in turn, affect marks. Once the feedback loop is joined, in other words, it continues.

In both first and second grade in the middle-class school, expectations also changed in a way to narrow the discrepancy between expectations and marks. The tendency for expectations to rise overshadowed the tendency for them to fall, however. The aggregate-level data suggest there is a buoyancy effect such that if a child did worse than expected at midyear, expectations at year-end tended to remain the same, and the mark was brought into line. If the child did better than expected, expectations were likely to rise while the mark remained the same. (In the working-class school, the limited evidence suggests that conduct expectations fell when the children received a lower mark than expected. The buoyancy effect appeared smaller or absent in the working-class school—but this conclusion is tentative.) The buoyancy effect may be a consequence of parents' expectations. Parents are the strongest source of influence on changes in first-grade marks in the middle-class school. Since the changes in marks there tend to be more in an "up" than in a "down" direction, and since most children who do poorly there are ones not expected by their parents to do poorly, parents' expectations may buoy up rather than push down grades overall.

Of those middle-class children whose expectations increased during first grade, over two-thirds were recruited from the group of children who did better than they had expected. Expectations responded vigorously— more vigorously than marks—to a discrepancy. The same finding appeared in second grade, where from 54% (arithmetic) to 72% (reading) of those whose expectations moved up apparently did so in response to an earlier positive discrepancy.

A significant portion of the dynamics of children's marks and expectations, then, can be accounted for in terms of prior expectation-mark discrepancies. Changes in both marks and expectations appear to be a consequence of a prior discrepancy between them. Change cannot be evaluated in terms of either prior marks or expectations alone, however, because either variable taken by itself produces no patterns. To say that marks do not affect children is incorrect, but to gauge the effect, one must also know what was expected. Expectations also have an effect, but here again the effect is relative. By the end of second grade the movement toward consistency observed both for marks and expectations led to a state where a significant number of children were capable of realistically anticipating the mark they were to receive. There was still considerable room for improvement in third grade, however, because the number of matches at the end of second grade was still far from 100%.

All of the data we have assembled are observational, but, by luck, something approximating a "natural" experiment occurred. Between first and second grades, it turned out, teachers' marking practices changed (an intervention). There was no significant agreement between marks children received at the end of first grade and at midyear second grade, and the average marks for reading and arithmetic declined. Expectations persisted to a significant degree over this same period, however. Children continued to hold the same expectations even when the target of their predictions was altered by the introduction of a new teacher with different marking standards. Under these conditions the correspondence between marks and expectations fell off at midyear second grade. An important finding, however, is that feedback effects for both marks and expectations took hold and significantly reduced the discrepancy between marks and expectations by the end of second grade. Thus, discrepancy-reduction effects of feedback operated, despite drastic changes in one of the peg-variables defining the discrepancy.

Drawing a parallel between this sequence of events and an intentional intervention is not completely straightforward. At the same time, possibilities for remedial intervention along such lines do exist. Most of the encouraging signs related to "intervention" appeared in the middle-class school, however, and not in the working-class school. Yet, even in the working-class school, children whose arithmetic and conduct marks increased over the year were disproportionately recruited from among those who did worse than they expected at midyear.

In general the same patterns of outcomes are seen for all three subjects and for both schools—with the exception of reading in the working-class school. There, no patterns emerged. What could explain this? The system used for reporting reading marks to working-class children was undoubtedly one reason why it was hard for them to understand and utilize feedback. But why very high expectations in reading persisted after low marks were awarded may, perhaps, be better understood from the style of teaching reading found in the working-class school. It was taught by using a great amount of individual reinforcement. Both the teacher and the aide spent part of each day in small group sessions with children doing reading exercises, and adults administered explicit positive reinforcement at a high rate. As a consequence of this teaching mode, children who performed relatively poorly and so captured more of the teacher's attention may actually have received more encouragement than better performers. If they took longer to learn, they would be in face-to-face interaction with the teacher longer to cover the same fixed number of units.

The result is that, day after day, poor-performing children probably received strong, positive, face-to-face feedback, especially if they were in Distar groups (half of the classrooms). Such feedback might completely swamp any negative feedback the children received in written form on the three isolated occasions during the school year when report cards were issued.

Also, working-class children may interpret positive verbal feedback literally and unconditionally because the sociolinguistic style of many working-class children often differs from the more middle-class linguistic background of their teachers. Other research in sociolinguistics and reinforcement with lower-class children suggests that a teacher's optimism and generally pleasant manner may stand out against a background of negative feedback from lower-class parents. When teaching children to do simple tasks, working-class parents tend to tell a child what he is doing wrong, i.e., "No, no, don't do that," whereas middle-class adults tend to reinforce what the child is doing correctly (Hess, Shipman, Brophy, and Bear, 1968). In light of this, face-to-face verbal reinforcement of children by teachers may have had different resonance for working-class than for middle-class children.

The apparent minimal effects of the mark-expectation discrepance on change in marks in reading for working-class children may be a consequence of conflict between the teacher's verbal and written feedback. Any person, child or adult, would attend more to feedback that is direct, immediate, unambiguous, and positive than to rare pieces of negative feedback. To do otherwise would be exceedingly maladaptive. The children's high expectations may exactly match what are perceived to be high daily evaluations in the classroom.

Should positive, face-to-face feedback be stopped or diminished? How can any young child be persuaded to practice and drill without considerable encouragement? These are difficult questions and, yet, to link excessive encouragement in the classroom with rigid marking practices, as is done in the working-class school, may be risky. At some point children with low capabilities must feel sharp dissonance when their beliefs about the high level of their skill in reading or arithmetic are contradicted. In first grade the dissonance may be manageable because neither children nor parents understand the marking practices very well and both may unconsciously shield themselves from disappointment by cloudy perceptions. But at some point children are made aware of their ineptitudes. Imagine how children must feel, for example, in third or fourth grade, when marks are low or failing and they realize that they have been "conned" in the classroom through the first three years of school by empty phrases.

Two big questions remain: (1) When, if ever, do working-class children's expectations become more realistic? (2) If their expectations do become more realistic, will strong causal effects emerge similar to those observed in the middle-class school? So far, causal effects are similar for children whose expectations are modest enough in arithmetic and in conduct to permit tests of hypotheses, but, for reading, too-high expectations persist despite highly negative feedback.

Parents' Expectations

In both schools parents tended to "play it safe." In each subject area the majority of parents forecast a "B." Teachers in the middle-class school also "played it safe," for they awarded mostly B's. Divergence between parents' expectations and marks were thus minimized. Not only did parents' and teachers' "see" the same overall distribution of marks in the middle-class school, but there was also notable agreement between them on a child-by-child basis for reading, arithmetic, and conduct over both first and second grades. Middle-class parents did seem able to identify children who would perform poorly or very well,. even as early as the first report card.

When middle-class parents' first-grade expectations were not correct, errors were in the direction of underestimating. By slightly underestimating how well a child would do, the parent voiced basic confidence in the child, yet allowed a margin for pleasant surprise. Middle-class parents, in other words, put themselves and their children in a social context where neutral or positive consequences were made likely at report card time.

Working-class parents, on the other hand, tended to overestimate their children's future performance in reading and arithmetic throughout first grade. The overestimation did not come about because parents held unduly high expectations—in fact, they held lower reading and arithmetic expectations than middle-class parents did. The shower of low reading and arithmetic marks on children's first report cards was just not anticipated by working-class parents; unlike the middle-class parents, they did not ''see'' the same distributions of marks as teachers in the school their children attended. The case-by-case matching between working-class parents' expectations and their children's marks was significant only when the overall mark distributions were most lenient (and, hence, similar to the parents' expectation distribution)—namely, for year-end reading and for conduct throughout first grade. The actual distributions of marks used by teachers in the middle-class school agreed well with what both middle-class and working-class parents anticipated.

Working-class parents may not have realized that so many first graders in the school their child attended got low marks. Later in first grade marks went up and therefore agreed somewhat better with parents' initial forecasts, so each parent may have been lulled into thinking that his child's first mark was an aberrant case rather than one instance of a general phenomenon.

Certainly parents in the middle-class school were much more aware of ''norms'' and more vocal on matters of school policy. One index of parents' involvement is the response rate in this research from the two sets of parents. For cohort S-1 in first grade, 92% of parents visited school during American Education week, and their expectations were sampled at the time of this visit. Frequently both mother and father visited. We were able to secure responses from only 74% of the working-class parents, even though we used trained interviewers who went to the children's homes (preceded by an introductory flyer carried home by the children) and who persisted through three call-backs. When we attempted to interview working-class parents by seeing those who came to school during American Education week, the response rate was less than 10%. The fact that middle-class parents were in close touch with school while working-class parents were not may partly explain why middle-class parents correctly anticipated the overall mark distributions teachers used while the working-class parents did not and, also, why teachers assigned higher marks in the middle-class schools—they know that they might hear from parents if they give a child a low mark.

A surprising result is that in no subject area in either school did individual parents' and children's expectations match significantly at the time of the first report card. In addition, middle-class parents' expectations did not match their children's expectations at any time in second grade. Children, therefore, obviously did not adopt their parent's expectations directly, and apparently the home environment did not lead parents and children to form the same expectations. A relationship between parents' and children's expectations should develop over time, however, because both sets of expectations tend to move toward the child's assigned marks.

There is a high correlation between middle-class parents' expectations in reading and in arithmetic, but no relation between parents' expectations for either of these areas and expectations for conduct. Middle-class parents thus demonstrate the compartmentalization of expectations for their children's school performance that Kohn (1969) would predict. They do not see classroom behavior—ability to sit still, to be docile, to be deferent—as being related to intellectual performance. The parents' grouping of reading and arithmetic together contrasts sharply with the way children categorize the two subjects. Children in both schools showed significant tendencies to expect different marks in reading and arithmetic.

Parents in the middle-class school showed a higher degree of consistency in their expectations from one year to the next than the consistency found either in teachers' marks or in children's expectations between years. The degree of year-to-year matching, even for parents, is not particularly strong, however. Parents, rather sensibly, tended to bring their second-grade expectations into line with their child's first-grade performance.

We have not yet reviewed the influence parental expectations have on children's performance. This can be done by observing the changes in children's performance resulting from the discrepance between parents' expectations and their children's prior performance. For middle-class children in first grade, highly significant movement of marks *both up and down* occurred in all three subject areas in precisely the fashion required to reduce the parents' prior expectation-mark discrepance. Over first grade the movement of marks toward consistency with parents' expectations appeared stronger than the movement toward consistency with the child's own expectations, particularly in cases of mark decline (best seen by looking at the four corner cells in the various tables that summarize "consistency movement" in marks).

The force of parents' expectations appears stronger than the force of children's expectations in first grade, but the reverse is true in second grade. The impact of a prior parental expectation-mark discrepance was considerably reduced in second grade (only that for reading attained significance), while the effect of the child's expectation-mark discrepance stayed about the same as in first grade. Why this is so is not clear.

That effects attributable to the children's discrepance continue while effects attributable to the parent's discrepance decline is one piece of evidence suggesting that the possible confounding between effects attributable to parents' and children's discrepances is not as serious a problem as might be feared. Two other observations also argue against substantial confounding: (a) the parental discrepance acted in part to *lower* marks, while the children's discrepance led to weak, possibly negligible, lowering effects; and (b) children's expectations were generally higher than parents' expectations, implying that any such confounding would be inexact and, therefore, attenuated.

We conclude this section by noting the role IQ played in determining parents' expectations. In the middle-class school 20 to 25% of the variation in parents' first-grade substantive area expectations can be accounted for by the child's IQ. The variance accounted for falls to about 10 to 15% in second grade. This decline is not surprising considering the change in information available to parents between first and second grades. Before the first report card, parents had to glean information from their children's actual behavior in order to form their expectations. By second grade they had already seen a series of report cards that told them directly about their child's performance. If parents then formed their expectations more on the basis of their child's mark history than on instances of actual behavior, they would be relying on highly contaminated information, from the perspective of IQ. Marks are influenced by everything from school marking policies to the teacher's attempts to motivate the children.

A much more puzzling and highly provocative observation is that IQ accounts for from 20 to 35% of the variation in white parents' reading and arithmetic expectations, irrespective of social class, and accounts for almost none of the variation in black parents' substantive area expectations in the working-class school. For some as-yet-unknown reason, these black parents either fail to pick up appropriate cues about their children's ability (as predicted by IQ) or avoid the utilization of the cues they have picked up when they form their expectations.

Sex Differences

The discovery of fascinating sex differences that exist even by first grade has emerged from a limited environmental framework. All teachers are female, for example, and almost all parents' views represent mothers' views. The possible sex differences are thus strictly circumscribed, and might better be called "sex differences, given the usual social restrictions on cross-sex interactions present in first grade."

There were almost no significant differences by sex in either children's expectations or in parents' (mostly mothers') expectations at any time in either school in first grade. This is surprising, given the well-documented higher failure rate for boys in reading. Most of the insignificant differences that appear are consistent with the social stereotypes that say girls will do better than boys in reading and conduct while boys will do better than girls in arithmetic.

Reading marks in both schools did not show a significant association with sex at midyear. By year-end, however, more boys than girls in the middle-class school got the poorer marks in reading, but this was not true in the working-class school. At no time was there any significant association between marks in arithmetic and sex in either school.

In conduct there were large sex differences at both midyear and year-end favoring girls in the working-class school. In the middle-class school the sex difference in conduct marks was not significant. Sex differences in conduct marks, therefore, are characteristic only of the working-class children, and this fact should be contrasted with the fact that there was a slight tendency for middle-class parents to expect poorer conduct from boys than from girls, while, surprisingly, working-class parents expected about the same performance in conduct from boys and girls. The expectations of middle- and working-class parents for boys and girls are at odds with what might have been predicted, for one would expect working-class parents to have more stereotypically sex-typed expectations for girls than middle-class parents have.

By second grade there were modest differences by sex in reading marks, with girls' marks exceeding boys'. No differences appeared for arithmetic. The strong tendency for girls to get better marks in conduct, noted in first grade, persisted. Also as in first grade, differences in expectations according to sex were practically nonexistent, except that parents had a slight tendency to expect their sons to get lower conduct marks than their daughters did.

Perhaps the most interesting sex differences in first grade are those in the correlations between IQ and conduct marks. Middle-class high-IQ girls tended to get better marks in conduct, but no such association was seen for middle-class boys. Just the opposite was found in the working-class school—there, IQ is significantly and strongly correlated with conduct marks for boys, but not for girls. There seems to be no immediate explanation for this intriguing sex difference in conduct-IQ correlations.

This sex difference in the correlations between IQ and conduct marks continued into second grade. Middle-class girls continued to exhibit small though significant (at midyear) negative correlations while boys displayed small and insignificant positive correlations.

Peer Ratings

Middle-class children's within-class peer ratings did not have much influence in the first two years of school. Children's expectations were completely unrelated to peer ratings. Marks showed small though reasonably consistent correlations with peer ratings. The timing of the observation periods for peer ratings (late in the school year) would allow children to utilize the teacher's in-class evaluations of their classmates, and, therefore, would account for the small mark correlations. The correlation seen in first grade between parents' expectations and their children's peer ratings all but disappeared by second grade. These middle-class children's expectations, from all signs visible in the present data, appeared to be insensitive to peer-group pressures.

Neither working-class children's expectations nor working-class parents' expectations were related to children's within-class peer ratings, but working-class children's marks did show a relationship to peer ratings in first grade. The observed interactions between peer ratings and race will not be pursued here because the data base is small, but it should be noted that peer ratings significantly predict performance in all three marking areas for children of one race or the other, if not both. A provocative question for the future is whether peers in the working-class school will increase their influence in second grade, and whether there will be race differences in this regard. What is perhaps most interesting about possible class differences are the different "significant others" in the two locales.

Standardized Achievement

Standardized achievement scores confirmed that children in the working-class school did not learn to read nearly as well as children in the middle-class school. The scores also confirmed that children's marks were sufficiently correlated with standardized achievement to allow careful generalization from discussion of marks to actual performance capabilities.

The only perplexing observation related to standardized achievement was the correlation of .07 between IQ and second-grade standardized reading achievement for the working-class school. Why this value is so low is unclear. It is unlikely that children's expectations can explain the low correlation, since IQ and children expectations have been unrelated in all data seen so far.

Effects of Absences

Strong and consistent correlations for working-class children appeared between marks and both lateness and absences. All during first grade, the child who was absent more was also apt to be the child who did poorly in reading and arithmetic. This association between absences and marks equals the association seen for IQ. In other words, knowing how often a child is absent is almost as useful a predictor of marks as knowing the child's IQ. This is a rather startling realization.

The comparable large correlations between performance and lateness are even more startling because the logical basis for such an association is not obvious. It is hard to see lateness itself as a direct cause of poorer performance, if we think in terms only of missed instructional time. The study time a child missed while absent might be used to explain the absence-mark correlation. It is mystifying why comparable correlations should appear for lateness, which involves substantially less "missed study time." Also, the negative impact of lateness on marks cannot be explained as a consequence of particular parental or children's expectations, since these bear no relationship to lateness. Parental expectations are correlated with absence, but not with lateness. Nor can it be explained by claiming that the children who are often absent are the same children who are often late, since the correlation between absences and lateness is quite low (r = .246). The interpretation is even further complicated by the lack of similar correlations in the middle-class sample. There, no absence-mark correlations were significant in first grade and only one out of six possible correlations was significant in second grade. (Lateness data were not available.)

The answer to why absence has such negative effects in one school and not in the other may be, simply, that the association is related to the lower variance of the middle-class absences scores. The lower correlations in the middle-class school could stem from restriction on the range of the absence variable (a purely artifactual effect), or the *reasons* for the restricted range of absence scores might themselves provide the appropriate explanation. That is, the cause for the reduced variance in the middle-class school may also provide the reason for the correlation difference. It is possible, for example, that it is the least competent children in the working-class school who lack the basic clothing necessities and who are likely to be kept home in inclement weather—almost no middle-class children are similarly influenced. Family differences in the ability to respond to inclement weather would explain the reduced variance (and lack of correlation) in the middle-class school and the correlation observed in the working-class school. The patterns of correlations and the reduced middle-class variance may also be explained if it is true that the poorest families experience the greatest number of health problems (and account for a disproportionate number of slow learners) and middle-class children experience fewer health problems.

Summary

Children in both schools have high expectations at the start. Middle-class children's expectations are only slightly too high, while working-class children's expectations are much too high. Parents in both places have more modest expectations than their children, but middle-class parents are more successful at prediction than working-class parents because they seem to know what the actual marking practices of the school are. Working-class parents' expectations would tend to be fulfilled if their children received marks comparable to marks given in the middle-class school.

In both schools, as far as we can tell, change either in children's marks or in their expectations comes about in response to modest discrepancies between children's expectations and their marks. When discrepancies are too large, as in the working-class school, feedback exerts little or no effect. Causal effects of parental expectation-mark discrepances were stronger than effects of children's discrepances in the middle-class school in first grade, but waned in second grade. The parents' discrepance, unlike the children's discrepance, accounted for downward changes in marks as well as upward changes. Since working-class parents were far off-target in predicting their children's first marks, part of the potential influence of their expectations may have been wasted.

Racial differences in expectations were minimal. This may reflect the long and unusually favorable integrated history of the particular school observed. The most provocative and, at this time, inexplicable racial difference is that black parents' expectations were unrelated to their children's IQ's while white parents in both schools apparently based their initial expectations to a large extent on their (accurate) perception of their child's IQ.

Appendix

As noted in Appendix A to chapter 2, the *Maryland Accountability Program Report, School Year 1973–74* provides data for third graders enrolled in the middle- and working-class schools that is comparable in some ways to the data we procured from school records. The middle-class third graders in the report are the same children as those in cohort S-1. The working-class third-graders in the report are from the cohort preceding cohort L-1 in the working-class school. Table A6.1 illustrates that the average "SAS" or IQ data for the two schools differ *more* in third grade than they did in first grade. In tables 3.1 and 5.1 we see that the middle-

Table A6.1

Third-Grade Achievement Data for Both Middle-Class and Working-Class Schools

	SAS*	Iowa Tests of Basic Skills Grade Level Equivalents			Predicted Grade Equivalents with SAS Controlled		
		Vocabulary	Reading	Mathematical Total	Vocabulary	Reading	Mathematical Total
Middle Class	113.1	4.50	4.60	4.30	4.35	4.45	4.33
Working Class	90.4	2.40	2.73	2.93	2.90	2.94	3.10

*Cognitive Abilities Test, Form 1, 1971. A "nonverbal subtest" involving figure classification, figure analysis, and figure synthesis where "SAS" means "Standard Age Score." The national average score for students of the same age is "100" and the standard deviation of the score is unknown. The actual number of third-graders in each school who were tested is also unspecified.

class average PMA IQ was 113.5, while the working-class average PMA IQ was 103.3. This difference may be due to cohort differences, testing differences, or sampling variability. A trend in the report data shows an almost constant average SAS score for older middle-class children, while the older working-class children show declining SAS scores. Thus the relatively small differences we saw in tested ability at the start of school become progressively larger as time passes. This trend may be due either to a widening of the gap between schools as the children grow older or to a monitoring of a consistent improvement of SAS scores for each successive cohort of working-class children.

Standardized achievement scores in reading and mathematics (Iowa Tests of Basic Skills) are almost identical to those we report from the middle-class cohort in table 4.13. The improvised grade-level equivalent score we reported in Table 5.11 is also comparable to the values reported here. When the grade-level equivalent scores are adjusted for SAS, the differences between the schools are slightly diminished. The performance levels of the children in the two schools, however, remain about one-and-one-half school grades apart, even with the adjustment. There seems little doubt that children in the middle-class school are converting school resources into attainment more efficiently than children in the working-class school.

Parental status is usually characterized as a separate resource in research on adolescents' status attainment. The present research leads us to take the view that it is more an interactive effect, that children from middle-class homes are experiencing a more efficient feedback process in first grade. At the start of school children in both places have above-average ability, outstanding school resources, parents with optimistic hopes, and no visible impediments to achievement. In the middle-class school, children are attuned to feedback, either directly or through their parents. In the working-class school, the basis for feedback may be mystifying if it is based, as it seems to be, more on absence than on ability (IQ).

CHAPTER 7

Retrospect, Prospect
—and Suspect

A set of questions was listed in chapter 1. Some of these we have already answered directly, in chapter 6. The first question concerned the expectations children had for themselves when they started school. To answer this question we found it necessary to simultaneously answer the sixth question: how does social class affect expectations? Children in both the middle-class and working-class schools had expectations that were, on the average, too high. There was an inverse relation between socioeconomic status and expectation level, however; we found that children from the lower status school had higher average expectations. In the middle-class school expectations were only slightly too high, while in the other school expectations were much too high.

The second question in chapter 1 inquired how children's early performance compared with expectations. We saw that at the time of the first report card there was no statistically significant match in any cohort between children's expectations and their marks. Children must have been surprised by the first marks they received. Middle-class children's average expectations were closer to the average marks they received than were those of working-class children, but, on a child-by-child basis, significant agreement between earliest expectations and marks was lacking in every cohort. This is not to say that all agreement was lacking, for it turned out, "by chance," that about one-third of the middle-class children's expectations agreed with their marks. One-third is not a statistically significant figure, however; a significant match would require that close to a majority of the children be correct. Substantial numbers of middle-class children were, nevertheless, accurate in their expectations for their first report cards, even though it may have been entirely fortuitous.

Almost all of the working-class children, on the other hand, were inaccurate. The working-class children received more D's than any other mark on their first report cards. When these low marks were compared with the children's very high expectations, we found that almost none of the children were correct.

We feel it would be a mistake to form firm conclusions about the third and fourth questions raised in chapter 1 (whether children's expectations affect early school performance and how expectations and performance level interact as feedback occurs) because of limitations on the data for working-class children. Our opinion at this time, however, is that children's expectations are causally efficacious if expectations are "in the ballpark." This opinion takes into account both the repeated documentation of effects of expectation-mark discrepances on subsequent marks in the middle-class school and, especially, the finding that working-class children's arithmetic marks showed significant discrepance-related movement. Working-class children's expectations for arithmetic were lower, on the average, than their expectations for reading, and therefore were more often closer to being realistic. Also, arithmetic marks were communicated in a more intelligible fashion than reading marks, so a more adequate test of the feedback hypothesis was possible, even though only a single time cycle was studied in the working-class school.

The story that unfolded in chapter 5 might have had a different theme if the modal mark in reading on the first report card for children in the working-class school had been a B instead of a D. To allow working-class children's initial expectations to bear fruit, it might have been preferable to assign marks more leniently at the start. Expectations of working-class children may be so badly undercut in first grade that they lose any potential they had for acting as a causal force.

The possibility of changing marking policies from one grade to the next in a way that capitalizes on the potential leavening force of expectations and at the same time gradually approaches objective evaluations does not seem out of place, especially in view of what actually occurred in the schools. In both schools marking policies in first grade, even though poles apart, were carried out with some fidelity. By second grade, however, teachers in both places began to act more independently of "official" marking policy. Teachers of middle-class children were unable to base their marks entirely on effort (correlations between marks and both standardized achievement and IQ increased), while teachers of working-class children were unable to mark entirely on the basis of ability (mark-IQ correlations declined substantially). The teachers were probably forced to reshape the marking policies according to the realities of situations in which they found themselves.

How can middle-class teachers give a child who is reading very well but not "trying hard" a C, and give another child, who reads poorly but seemingly tries harder, a B? By the same token, working-class teachers cannot fail every other child in a class, even if all their performances are poor. Giving negative evaluations continuously in an educational setting, be it kindergarten or college, causes students to absent themselves either physically or psychologically. In sum, it appears that policies as implemented in both schools by necessity become more similar as time passes.

Events in first grade, however, may condition children's reactions to evaluations so that they do not perceive later policies to be equivalent, even if the policies actually are much the same. Rather than letting marking policies wander about in ways children, parents, and teachers may be explicitly unaware of, it might be better to monitor marking policy closely. It then might be possible to institute policies designed to extract the maximum beneficial effect from children's initially high expectations.

In completing this flashback to chapter 1, we remember that the fifth and sixth questions there focused on social context and ascriptive characteristics. The broad social context, the relatively narrow and immediate context of significant others, and the child's sex, race, and IQ all seemed potentially important candidates among the variables we could study.

The broad social context in terms of average socioeconomic status was related to average expectation level, but this relationship was the only one uncovered. Sex, race, IQ and parents' expectations all turned out to be essentially unrelated to children's initial expectations. The infrequent differences that appear were small in magnitude and do not warrant any statement of important differences on these dimensions. We do not yet know what produces children's initial expectations, so we do not know whether the lack of differences arises from the sexes and races being similar on some macrosociological dimension (such as an underlying value) or on some microsociological dimension (such as experiencing certain types of face-to-face interactions).

Another way to examine social context is to examine the rationality of parents' expectations from the children's point of view. Working-class parents' expectations, for example, were accurate in the sense that they were lower than middle-class parents' expectations, and also in the sense that, by the end of the year, parents' expectations and their children's marks in reading did coincide to a significant degree. Parents' expectations and initial marks, however, were far apart. The minimal influence working-class parents' expectations had on changes in their children's performance in first grade might be ascribed to the actual utility of the parent's initial expectation—being low from the child's point of view. Children either consciously or unconsciously must attune themselves to social reality. The working-class parent demonstrated that parental reality and school reality were disjunct by not correctly anticipating what the first report card would show. For a child to ignore the parent's opinion in such a setting makes sense.

Middle-class parents, on the other hand, tended to have expectations in line with what actually happened. Middle-class children apparently paid attention to their parents' initial expectations, furthermore, for those expectations were a stronger influence on performance than any other variable we studied. Since those expectations were reliable in the sense that they agreed significantly with the initial feedback the child received from teachers, they could help the child in defining social reality. The differential influence of parents in the two schools can be seen, in view of these facts, as the consequence of rather sensible adjustments on the part of their children.

The seeming reliance of white parents on cues related to IQ in forming their expectations and the lack of a similar reliance by black parents *could* have led to racial differences in children's performance if working-class parents in general (and white working-class parents in particular) had turned out to be reliable sources of information for their children. The working-class child, whether black or white, actually got confusing signals from parents, however, because both sets of parents' expectations were too high.

Working-class children probably also got mixed signals from teachers, since day-to-day classroom evaluations disagreed with report card evaluations. To try to get all children to perform up to Distar or other fixed curricular standards probably required teachers to reinforce poorly performing children more than the more capable children, as mentioned earlier. The feedback the working-class child received from the adults around him, whether parents or teachers, was likely to be contradicted by the written evaluations the child received.

Peers in the working-class school did have some influence. Perhaps this is because teachers and parents, if they are unreliable informants, recede as significant others and leave a "social influence vacuum" the peers fill. How children are affected by peers and how peer influence waxes and wanes is a topic of considerable sociological interest, but for children as young as those studied in this research, the literature on this topic is sparse.

We know peers are influential in adolescence, when children try to establish identity and social independence (Coleman, 1961; Entwisle, 1975). The so-called "adolescent crisis" in part denotes a time when peers begin to dominate the circle of significant others. Such an adolescent crisis may be essential for adequate functioning as an adult—the period of childhood must come to a decisive end. A premature crisis of a similar kind occurring much earlier in the child's life, however, say, in first grade, could be severely dysfunctional. By the time they are six or seven years old, children are still so incompletely socialized themselves that they do not possess the resources adequate to underwrite the socialization of other children. In other words, relying on peers' judgments of competence is hazardous if peers have little rational basis for judging.

Causal Impact

A major finding of this study is that both children's marks and children's expectations shifted over time to minimize the differences between them. Causal effects of discrepancies were clearly documented throughout first and second grades in the middle-class school. The skewed mark and expectation marginal distributions in the working-class school hampered analyses for that school, but all available indications suggest that, to the extent feedback was effective, it operated in a similar fashion in the working-class school.

We also demonstrated the causal impact of the discrepancy between the parents' initial expectations and their children's early marks. In the middle-class school, children's marks in first grade tended to change so as to reduce the preceding parental discrepancy. Apparently children worked harder when their parents expected more, and relaxed when their parents expected less. The causal impact of parents' expectations was considerably reduced in second grade, after parents' expectations themselves had moved substantially toward consistency (minimization of the earlier discrepancy) between first and second grades. That is, the parents' discrepancy had less impact after parents had an opportunity to modify their expectations in light of their children's mark history. In the working-class school the parental mark-expectation discrepancy was also significantly effective in changing children's reading marks over first grade.

These causal effects of expectations were documented in naturalistic settings within the normal operation of the schools involved, and were not produced by artificial or experimental manipulations. For the first time a set of intuitively reasonable effects related to young children's expectations has been uncovered in a natural setting. The documentation of such effects is strong evidence for the construct validity of our expectation measure. Most convincing, as far as validity is concerned, is the internal consistency of findings—the replication from cohort to cohort and from school to school in how expectations behaved. The likelihood of repeatedly observing such effects by chance is negligible.

The force of the causal impact of expectations also warrants notice. The excess number of children whose marks changed in accordance with previous discrepancies is not large—never more than 10 percent. On the other hand, 10 percent of all students represents a sizeable number of children to be influenced over any one semester, especially since the changes occur in reading and/or arithmetic, the two subjects at the core of the grade-school curriculum.

A Broader View

Considerable light has been shed on the basic questions that prompted this research. In the rest of this chapter we take a broader and deeper view of the findings by asking additional questions bearing on theoretical and policy issues. The questions are difficult to formulate because some of the most provocative issues were not foreseen, but we think it important to come to grips with such issues in print, since our research findings imply considerably more than we have yet acknowledged. We have an advantage over the reader both in enunciating the issues and in reflecting upon them because we have more and richer information available to us in the form of actual data and subjective impressions than is contained in the six preceding slender chapters.

It is important to emphasize again that every statement in this chapter and in the preceding chapters carries a strong caveat: *only two schools have been studied*. We hope that what we have seen in these two schools is representative of what happens in other middle-class and working-class schools, but it may not be. There simply is no sure way to judge. The demographic data on the income, housing, and education levels of the families served by the schools (reported in chapter 2) do convey the impression that the schools are "typical" middle-class and working-class schools. On the other hand, black or white children may behave differently toward one another in other schools, since few integrated schools have had as long a history of having approximately equal numbers of children of both races as the working-class school studied here. Also, what happens in Baltimore may or may not be a good barometer of what to expect elsewhere, even in Washington or Philadelphia, much less in smaller communities or points off the eastern seaboard. We will not qualify every statement in what follows with a warning about the samples' limitations. This survey has been selective, intensive, longitudinal, and preliminary, and the reader has now been cautioned sufficiently.

POSSIBLE HEURISTICS

This research is almost entirely descriptive. The first stage of description is to separate and clarify independent and dependent variables. Children's expectations were first selected from among the many variables that could have been studied. The measures for expectations and measures for alternate or supplementary variables (such as the discrepance variables) were developed. These activities started in 1969.

A second stage, obviously, was to rank the selected variables by importance. Which were unimportant? Which were spurious? Which variables, of the important ones, were relatively more important? Second stage exploratory work called for rough analyses such as those used throughout this book—cross-tabulations, zero-order correlations, visual inspection of differences across subgroups, and the like. The work of this stage also involved controlling some variables to prevent them from obscuring or distorting how other variables acted. We looked, for example, at the relation between children's expectations and marks when IQ was controlled.

Only after extensive exploration and after a sizeable data base has accumulated can one proceed, gingerly, to a further stage, and we cannot yet do this. The final stage is one where full structural models are developed and tested. The hope then is to specify both the *nature* and *magnitude* of the relationships among a surviving set of variables. If we could now write a set of equations showing how feedback affects expectations over time, for instance, or if we could specify whether parameters in the equations explaining children's performances were the same or different in the two social milieux, we would be at the third stage. We are not there, however. The visual models presented at the ends of chapters 3, 4, and 5 represent a synthesis of the preliminary findings (stages one and two), based on the three cohorts. These visual diagrams are only heuristics, and cannot be even a first step toward stage three. We present them merely for convenience, to help us and the reader keep in mind the major findings.

The visual models are not comprehensive, for not all the variables or relationships discussed in the text appear in the diagrams. Some variables did not survive initial screening, and were intentionally omitted. For example, the self-esteem variable for middle-class children was omitted because it was not meaningfully related to anything else in first grade. Other significant and highly interesting relationships could not be portrayed at all. There is no portrayal of the undermatching between children's expectations for reading and arithmetic, for instance, even though this phenomenon appeared consistently in both schools, and, we believe, is one of our most important findings. To portray this relation would have required a diagrammatic distinction between undermatching and a negative correlation as well as arrows between diagrams.

Other relations were excluded from the diagrams simply because we thought they were produced by relations already included in the diagrams.

For example, no direct relationships were diagrammed between children's marks and expectations in second grade.

Use of overcomplicated notation for greater completeness of these diagrams would have defeated their purpose—condensing information so the reader could move easily back and forth between schools and among performance areas. The nature of the structural relations between variables and the precise specification of the variables are not yet known.

Fortunately some decisions to include or exclude variables were not final because the raw data for refabricating those variables are still available. Other decisions to exclude variables were perilous, however, because the decisions were made before the project was begun; some variables were excluded a priori. For instance, we do not know parents' precise occupations, teachers' IQs, or children's health status. Such variables might be interesting, but the raw data do not exist to check them.

Constraints placed on research by a priori decisions are not peculiar to this project, of course, but they are an especially crucial—and cruel—feature of long-term longitudinal projects. The consequences of sampling aberrations, instrument bias and unreliability, theoretical blind spots, and the like are more serious for longitudinal than for cross-sectional research because the same operations are repeated over and over by the same researchers on the same sample(s). We do not wish to frighten the reader with these comments, we just want the reader to reflect on them as he looks at the broader issues addressed by the findings.

Expectations: Performance, Levels, Sources, and Crystallization

Ultimately the value of research resides in its utility, whether it can explain findings not previously explained or join findings previously seen as disjunct. This research has already given promise of some utility, especially in terms of the construct validity of its major variables. Expectations were linked with performance in intuitively reasonable ways several times. It is encouraging in the same way to find explanations for why IQ could have such different impact on performance in different social milieux (compare the differential sources of parental expectations with the corresponding differential impact of IQ on standardized achievement). It is also encouraging to find underlying compatability between expectations as a theoretical construct and other theoretical constructs like Rotter's concepts of internal and external control. What follows is a review of some of the

implications of expectations per se; after that we relate expectations as a
construct to other theoretical constructs.

Schools leave an indelible imprint on a child, but precisely how do
children form ideas about their own ability and how do these ideas shape
their earliest academic attainments? What are the dynamics of "tricycle-
age" educational attainment? These questions have overriding interest because, as mentioned in chapter 1, many signs point toward stability in
achievement levels after about age nine. Third-grade achievement not only
reflects what has happened but predicts what will happen as far in the
future as the kind of occupational field the child will enter.

How children were "imprinted" as young scholars in this study depended on where they started school. The role children's and parents'
expectations played within the two school settings was different, but only
rarely could we unequivocally attribute school differences to any specific
factor (differences in social class, race, IQ, school marking policies, or
neighborhood).

It was hardly a surprise that children learned to read and do arithmetic
considerably better in the middle-class school than in the working-class
school. Social class differences consistently forecast achievement differences in the earliest school years not only in this research, but almost
without exception. The differences in reading achievement, however, were
certainly larger than we foresaw in view of either the above-average IQ
composition of the student bodies in both schools or the high quality
of staff and resources in the working-class school.

We still do not understand exactly what produced such differences.
The data suggest part of the explanation resides in the usefulness of the
feedback given the child. The net effect of the different roles played by
parents, peers, and teachers in the two places was to provide reliable
feedback about performance in one place and a set of confusing signals in
the other. If early feedback is wrong or irrelevant, the child's "cognitive
map" about school may be distorted, and it may be difficult to correct the
map later.

Children in the two schools acted differently and were treated differently in terms of expectations. Children were not "good" at guessing
their first marks in either school if the criterion of statistical significance is
used. On the other hand, a sizeable proportion of middle-class children
were correct, even if fortuitously so. It was not until the end of the second
grade, in fact, that even middle-class children displayed better-than-chance
ability to anticipate their marks in the three major marking areas. But

feedback in terms of marks given to middle-class first graders was not at all like the feedback given to working-class first graders, so most middle-class children were close if not actually correct in their expectations. Middle-class children were eased gently into the school system because their disappointments were modulated. Working-class children, by contrast, were baptized by fire. They were marked so severely on the first report card that, in reading, close to half of them got the poorest mark. This abrasive introduction to school was combined with the fact that its harshness was almost totally unexpected by both the children and their parents. The expectation-performance relations for them must be cloudy. One would expect the motivational potential of marks to be severely undercut.

To gain understanding of why children differ in their reactions to schooling, one must look in some detail at children's early school experiences *from their point of view*. A high proportion of all children expect to do well. Depending on how marks are assigned, however, it may be relatively easy or almost impossible for children to meet their goals. We suggest that programs attempting to compensate for social class differences (like Headstart and Upward Bound) have proved remarkably barren in part because the programs do not engage the child.

Part of the reason for large differences in achievement may lie in how social rewards are defined for the child. To develop sources of motivation within the self, so-called intrinsic motivation, a child needs to set realistic goals and have some reasonable chance of achieving those goals. The confusing feedback the working-class children in this study received, whether from parents or school, must make what they can do to achieve their goals a mystery to them—and, added to this, their goals were unrealistic.

The present discussion is part of a recurrent theme: reinforcement or rewards are defined by the receiver. The size of a reward is meaningless except insofar as it relates to what is expected. Social rewards like marks are reinforcing, or not reinforcing, because they are wedged into a matrix of expectations built up from earlier interpersonal contact. One child who gets a B may burst into tears; another child who gets a B may jump for joy. Teachers know this from experience, but it remains a hard act to manage.

EXPECTATION LEVEL

This research specifies what young children's expectations actually are when they begin school, something hitherto unknown. Some social analysts have thought poor children were already discouraged when they started school. Our data say this is not true. In the working-class school some of the children were very poor but their expectations were extremely high. In fact, the vast majority of the children (64% of the 300 or so children) expected to get the highest possible mark in reading. This is true whether children were white and middle-class or black and relatively poor. This finding is of considerable interest in itself, for it vitiates a good bit of speculation about the damaging self-views of minority-group or less privileged children when they start school.

How did these high initial expectations arise? We suggested earlier that until the children enter school their expectations have been largely confirmed. The process of maturation alone assures children of regular improvement in performance at a wide variety of tasks. Since children implicitly evaluate current performance against their own past history of similar performances, repeated success is assured. In the family there is little social comparison. The four year old can not expect to perform as well as an older sibling. The preschool child's social reference group does not include substantial numbers of children his own age or persons who are of a different race or social class. Until the beginning of school, the process of social comparison is not very discriminating. Only after the child enters school does the process of social comparison begin in earnest.

A child's optimistic expectations at the start of school can provide a bulwark to support and encourage the acquisition of competent behaviors if evaluations do not completely contradict expectations. Our data suggest that children, rather sensibly, pull their expectations in line with their performance if given a reasonable opportunity to do so, i.e., if the distance between expectations and performance is not too large. If, as in the working-class school, differences are extreme—most children expected A's and received D's—the psychologically self-preserving response is to discount the evaluation, and this is what seemed to happen.

An obvious question is: When children start school, what should their expectation level ideally be? To us the optimal goal seems to be for children to have expectations that assist them in performing consistently at the highest level at which they can perform with comfort. No one expectation level is appropriate for all children—the differential abilities of children assure us of that.

The optimization problem is made more prickly by each child's having expectations in several areas. For any given child the optimum levels are not necessarily equivalent for reading and arithmetic. In fact, data from both schools suggest arithmetic is marked harder, so expectations for arithmetic should, perhaps, be more modest than those for reading. Optimization might require expectations and marks to match in two of the three areas while expectations exceeded marks in the third area.

Nothing is known about optimum expectation levels, but one point is clear: evaluations indicating performance far below expectations signify punishment. If children's expectation levels are unrealistically high, as was true for working-class first graders, feedback is consistently punishing. The consequences of extremely punishing feedback, at least as far as we have been able to trace them, are either null or not currently evident. Low marks did not reduce the working-class first graders' high expectations, and their high expectations did not improve the low marks. Whether the punishing feedback is ignored, distorted, or repressed we do not know. Young children are like other human beings though, and probably shield themselves from unpleasantness. Since physical escape is impossible—children must go to school and must learn to read and to do arithmetic—children probably resort to psychological escape. They seemed to ignore extremely negative feedback and not process it. In this regard it is important to note than working-class children's expectations were least extreme for arithmetic and that expectations in arithmetic did affect their arithmetic performance. If children have expectations that are too high when they start school, this may lead to a lack of feedback effects, which in turn may lead to less effective learning. A child's behavior being too far off the target may simply baffle the child altogether and prevent the use of feedback.

Very high expectations that are not met could seriously interfere with learning in first grade because cues that signal to the child how to change are part of the feedback being ignored. As time passes, unrealistically high expectations, if they persist, may become severely dysfunctional. Oppressive feelings of defeat could occur if over and over the child does more poorly than expected. Eventually the child must become discouraged because he will not be allowed to ignore what is happening indefinitely; at some point failure must be acknowledged. Others (Brookover et al., 1962, 1964, 1965, 1967; Cohen, 1972; Cohen and Roper, 1972) have shown that older children's expectations can be very low. At some intermediate age between first grade and junior high school (the age of children in the other studies) children apparently readjust their expectations.

Working-class children's average marks improved a great deal over the year, but the children who first received D's and then improved to C's or received C's and then improved to B's very likely still did not attain their initial expectation. One consequence may be that a mark, even though it has considerably improved, fails to reinforce the student's extra effort. It is a better mark but the child may not perceive it as a reinforcement because his expectations have not diminished.

A child whose initial level of expectations is too low, on the other hand, may suffer relatively benign consequences. We have seen that expectations bounce up to equal performance. If a child's initial expectations are too low and they are not confirmed, the damage appears negligible. (This statement may be true only early in the school career, because later the child with low expectations, like those in the Cohen studies, may act to make them come true.) With young children it looks as though low expectations do not depress children's performances—the self-fulfilling prophecy is not fulfilled in these instances.

SOURCES OF EXPECTATIONS

Young children's expectations were not based, even in part, on the child's intellectual ability (IQ); neither were they based on parents' ideas of what their children could do. So far neither the racial group a child belongs to nor sex seem to explain initial expectations. These sources of expectations and others examined in this book have not gone very far toward answering unequivocally the question of where children's initial expectations came from. We suggested children's high expectations might arise from their preschool observation of their own maturing capabilities, but this is a hypothesis, not a finding.

It may actually be more important to discover how children who typically do less well in school form their initial expectations than to discover this for those who are average or above-average achievers. Being average or above almost guarantees the child's expectations will be "in the ballpark"—given the typical high levels of expectations. At the moment, however, we have no way of knowing whether good or poor students form their expectations in similar ways.

EARLY CRYSTALLIZATION

This research was sparked by many ideas, an outstanding one being that children's expectations might crystallize early in their school careers and be resistant to change thereafter. If this were true, then remedial efforts later in the life cycle might be ineffective (as has often been seen). Rist's (1970) observation that children were pigeonholed by kindergarten teachers in the first eight days of school suggested how expectations could be made to crystallize early. What does our research say about early crystallization?

For the middle-class school about 50 percent of the children held the same expectation from any one time period to the next, whereas about 40 percent would have been expected to do so by chance. This suggests that approximately 12 percent of the children may continuously hold the same expectation over the first two years of school compared to the roughly 6 percent who would be expected to do so by chance. Thus, while some "statistically significant" crystallization is present, it is not pronounced. Furthermore, the relatively stable percentage of children who persisted in their expectations from any one time to the next suggests that initial levels are no more potent than subsequent levels. If children changed their expectations, they were about as likely to persist in holding the new expectation as they were to persist in holding the initial expectation.

In the working-class school a higher proportion (about 65%) of the children maintained the same expectation from midyear to the end of first grade, but the observed percentages did not significantly exceed those expected by chance. Case-by-case, then, there was not significant crystallization in the working-class school in a statistical sense, even though a relatively large proportion of matches did occur.

The observation that expectations do not crystallize early directly contradicts statements like the following by Mussen, Conger, and Kagan (1963): "The child who enters school with a desire to do well is likely to develop into the adult who is concerned with intellectual competence." Our data flatly contradicts such a statement if "desire to do well" is translated as "high expectations." Early expectations are simply too inconsistent to allow for such long-range predictions. The sharp contrast between the high expectations of children and low parental involvement (concern) in the working-class school also throws doubt on the basis of such statements.

Some recent evidence points to a crystallization effect in *teachers'* expectations, however. In experiments by Feldman and Allen (1974), when a young tutor observed a good performance in his tutee to start with, his final evaluation of the tutee was higher than if the same good performance was observed later. That is, some tutees did well in the first half of a series of lessons and did poorly in the second half. Other tutees did the reverse, poorly first and then well later. *First* evaluations by the tutors tended to persist even when performance changed. Tutees who improved were perceived to be still performing at their initial low level and vice versa. One initial good or poor performance can thus cause many subsequent baseless positive or negative evaluations. If teachers' expectations crystallize as early as this experimental evidence and Rist's (1970) observational evidence suggest, then teachers' expectations in the earliest school days may etch a picture that is hard to erase. They may give several similar but inappropriate marks, to which children's expectations eventually converge.

Evidence from the present study supports Feldman's and Allen's (1974) experimental study yet simultaneously contradicts its "logical" extension to an indelible picture. The evidence is that there was significant matching between the marks teachers assigned to the children within grades in the middle-class school while there was no significant matching between the marks assigned in first grade and those assigned in second grade. The consistency of marks within a grade suggests that crystallization of teachers' expectations may be operative. Teachers' initial evaluations did persist throughout one school year. The lack of consistency between years, however, indicates that the persistence of marks within one grade stems from a factor such as a primacy effect and not from "objective" data. The lack of any significant matching between years indicates that the first-grade teacher's picture was erased by the second-grade teacher. Although the effect of the crystallization of teachers' expectations *within* grades may be indelible, the possibility of a long-term effect is made less worrisome by the lack of an effect between years. From this point of view the move into second grade, with a change in teachers, may be well timed.

Rists's observations, on the other hand, revealed between-year effects. The status hierarchy that developed among the children he observed in kindergarten persisted through the end of second grade. Since Rist's supporting data pertained to lower-class children while our nonsupporting data concerned middle-class children, this difference at present cannot be satisfactorily resolved.

Expectations and Personal Control

Over the last decade the sociological and psychological literature has bulged with studies on "sense of control."* Rotter's (1966) notion of internality and externality hit a particularly resonant note with sociologists whose traditions draw upon structural explanations of alienation and anomie. Efficacy has turned up as a variable in one sociological study after another, the best-known instance being the efficacy questions in the Coleman report (1966). In that report items such as the one inquiring whether the respondent felt "luck mattered more than hard work" predicted more unique variance in school performance than variables like integration status or school quality.

No one, however, seems to have looked to see how sense of control or feelings of efficacy develop in the first place. Just as self-expectations have been studied up to now only in their full-blown state in older children, so also the enormous literature on sense of control does not describe how sense of control begins or what its sociological roots may be. The present research has definite implications for the development of personal control, for control is conceptually closely related to expectation level.

The basic notions of internal and external control can be represented as the slope of lines A and B respectively in figure 7.1. Line A represents the model assumed by persons who view performance or achievement as

*This discussion draws heavily on ideas suggested by Feld (1975).

Figure 7.1
Geometric Representation of Internal and External Control

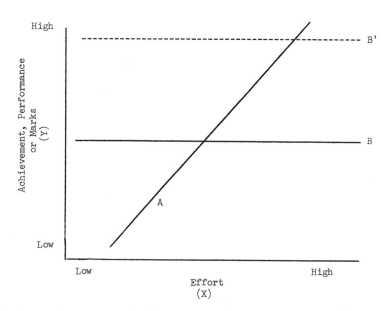

being contingent upon the effort expended. The person who works hard can expect to do well; persons who work little can expect to do poorly. Such persons view events as being at least partly responsive to their internal control. Line B represents the model assumed by persons who view performance as being independent of effort. They feel that no matter what they do their achievement or performance is unaffected. External forces control what will befall them. The two models represent the degree to which people perceive events as being contingent upon their own actions. (The models could easily be made more complex—nonlinear, for example—but to no purpose here.)

The role of expectations in these models is clear: given a model such as A (that for an internal control individual), expectations are the individual's predictions for level of achievement in relation to effort. In this sense expectations are the predicted level of achievement the person holds as a standard until comparison of this expected achievement with his actual achievement is possible. In our research children held their expectations from the time of formation until the time the report cards were issued, at which time they were able to compare their actual and expected performance.

Expectations play a relatively minor role in the day-to-day operation of the cognitive structures for models A and B shown in figure 7.1. Expectations play a much more prominent role, however, in both the original development of those structures and in their modification once they are developed. To illustrate the role expectations might play in the development of cognitive control sturctures, we will speculate a little on how sense of control develops.

Children's beginning attempts to discover a control function appropriate for themselves might consist of a set of trials in which, after noticing the effort they are expending, they guess at an appropriate control function from which to derive expectations (a random guess at first). The child, for example, exerts high effort (an x value) and then tries to guess the likely achievement (a y value). Next the child monitors actual performance. Finally, he uses the discrepance between the expected y value and the actual y value (performance) to improve the "guessing" rule. It is the attention given to the discrepance between the expected and the actual performance that allows alteration of the prediction rule so the next prediction of y from x is better. This sequence of events could be repeated many times. Each time the child would note effort level, formulate an expectation, and then observe the actual level of achievement that occurred. Eventually the child should develop a reasonably specific control function, for example line A in figure 7.1, consisting of many observed and corrected (x, y) points.

CONTROL AND SOCIAL CLASS

The operation of a similar iterative approximation procedure in the working-class school we observed would produce a model more like B, however, because expectations were maintained at an unrealistically high level. Somehow the children maintained high expectations no matter what degree of effort they felt themselves expending and no matter how discrepant their actual performance was in comparison with their previous expectations. They may have misread their actual performance, or not recognized its significance, or even have been rewarded for not discovering the correspondence between level of effort and level of achievement. Whatever forces children to form consistently high expectations will also force them to develop the control function diagrammed as B' in figure 7.1. Since they do not formulate lower expectations (i.e., the discrepance is ineffective), they cannot develop control functions that require them to modify (lower) their expectations. As a result they develop an *external* control function that produces high performance expectations irrespective of effort—subjectively, all levels of effort are linked to the same (high) expected performance, as noted in the Coleman report.

Children in the middle-class school, by contrast, apparently developed a control function like model A rather quickly. In fact they may have started school with such a function already under construction. Changes in expectations that moved these children toward consistency with marks represent an adjustment in the slope (and/or intercept) of the control function. Similarly, a change in marks that moves marks toward expectations causes the child to adjust the slope (and/or intercept) of the control function.

If middle-class children have a reasonably accurate control function when they start school, they may derive it from two sources. Either they have generalized from control curves developed previously for other similar activities, or they have been socialized explicitly to have such curves. The middle-class ethic underlying sayings such as "You can do it if you try," "Nothing ventured, nothing gained," or "If at first you don't succeed, try, try again" could produce socialization practices that directly lead young middle-class children to have such curves.

The theoretical link to Rotter's notion of control provides a fortuitous payoff from this research because it suggests a program for intervention in schools where children's expectations are too high. The discussion above suggests, surprisingly, that one might disregard expectations in interventions designed to produce realistic expectations. A program that makes it obvious to children that their performance in school depends on how hard they are willing to work and then gets children to evaluate realistically how hard they are working may have the desired outcome. By making it clear to them that average marks result from moderate effort and high marks require high effort, instructors could directly coach children to form a sense of internal control and thereby also assist them in forming realistic expectations. The emphasis on effort may seem a bit overdone, but this kind of program does not have the drawbacks of a program expressly designed to lower high expectations. In fact, the emphasis on effort in first grade was exactly what the middle-class school provided.

The foregoing discussion resolves some paradoxes, for it suggests how high expectations can be dysfunctional and how lower-class children could simultaneously have high expectations and a low sense of control. In fact, the developmental approach taken in this book and the specific findings that have emerged allow a sensible integration of previously inconsistent sets of findings concerning aspirations and control.

Control, efficacy, and expectations are important because they are related to early achievement behavior. In turn, early achievement is important because it is a stable personal attribute that predicts both later achievement behavior and eventual status attainment. We have begun to put a finger, we hope, on what leads to early achievement behavior. Plainly, high desire and competence are not necessarily connected—

neither middle-class or working-class children in this study were successful at predicting first marks. Too high a desire, furthermore, may undercut both the child's actual success and the child's perception of his ability to improve his performance.

The association between desire and success is complex, and is probably contingent upon the social milieu of the child. The present research shows that contingencies in one school were better adapted for producing personally experienced success in first grade than were contingencies in another school. A simplistic solution, then, like getting all children to expect or to desire to do well, is far off the mark. As far as we can tell, in fact, such a "remedy" would backfire.

Race and Expectations

The scholarly literature has more than its share of mushy thinking about expectations of lower-class and minority-group children, especially concerning how the expectations of such children operate to affect performance in mixed-race settings.

First, judging from the disappointing results of research using such measures, "global self-esteem" may be a meaningless concept. Global estimates of self-esteem simply do not predict school performance. In contrast, measuring the academic self-image does predict school performance (see Brookover et al., 1962, 1964, 1965, 1967), possibly because children's expectations focus on particular activities acted out among a particular set of people.

It is hardly surprising that a young child can, at one and the same time, realize that he is physically attractive, poor at playing ball, and good at arithmetic, or that he is good at playing ball with other first graders and poor when he plays with older children in his neighborhood sandlot. To try to find a touchstone for global self-esteem may be a fruitless endeavor in general, but it is an especially fruitless effort with young children. Global self-esteem could accrue over a lifetime of experiences. If self-esteem does develop by accumulation, first and second graders may be too young to have had the necessary exposure to a broad domain of experiences where they have been evaluated in comparative terms. We have argued that, most likely, young children's experiences in the family have been noncomparative, positive, and largely encouraging, making high expectations the rule. To imagine a socialization system that has the opposite effect, namely the effect of creating low expectations in preschool children, is to imagine a social system in the process of extinguishing itself.

Our data show that blacks do not hold themselves in low regard or look for failure when they start school. Other careful research also concludes that blacks do not typically hold low self-expectations. Rosenberg and Simmons (1971), for example, reported (also for a Baltimore sample) that black children did not have low self-esteem if they were in consonant or protective settings. The working-class school we studied is probably "protective" for blacks (despite its being integrated) because it has a long and successful integration history.

Minority-group children may be, and often are, unaware of society's low evaluation of the group to which they belong. Apparently young children have not yet internalized the social stigmas applied to their racial group. Working-class children in this study had higher expectations for success in school than middle-class children, and black working-class children's expectations turned out to be just as high as their white classmates'. We certainly did not find low expectations to be characteristic of lower-status children.

Contrary to notions often voiced, the way to improve the school performance of groups with educational deficits (like blacks or other minorities) does *not* seem to be to raise children's expectation levels. Children in the present study appeared to do poorly not because they thought they would do poorly, at least in first grade, but for other reasons, some of which are still unclear. In fact our findings indicate raising expectations would be exactly the wrong course to take. Children from the working-class school performed more poorly than those in the middle-class school but generally held expectations that were far too high. Unrealistically high expectations may be part of their handicap.

Such a finding about expectation levels contradicts what the "great society" thinkers of the 1960s supposed. Disadvantaged children, the thinking went, had a low sense of control because they knew that their reference groups had little control over resources or power in the larger society. Furthermore, children supposedly adopted these low expectations and acted upon them so as to fulfill the prophecy of low attainment. Our analysis suggests the opposite. With first graders, at least, expectations being too low definitely is not the problem. Almost all the working-class children interviewed in this study, whether black or white, started school with very high expectations. These expectations were so high that it was impossible to fulfill them. In the working-class school the system was not geared for fulfilling high expectations, even for a few children. In fact the system was not geared to fulfill even modest expectations.

The notions that "high expectations" are universally good and that "raising expectations" will make things better are absolutely contradicted by what we have observed, at least for young children. Children with unreasonably high expectations apparently insulated themselves from mark feedback, and marks, in turn, displayed insulation by not responding to excessively high expectations.

Whether feedback is "high" or "low," "good" or "bad," can be decided only when one knows a child's desired performance level. A high expectation linked to an average performance has very different consequences from a low expectation linked to an average performance. The discrepance, in other words, is the key, at least early in the game. If the discrepance is positive (performance exceeds expectation) or negative and small, the consequences for performance are good. If positive, the child has merely to attune himself psychologically to his own success by making an upward cognitive leap—something children have little trouble doing. If the gap is slightly negative, the odds are good that the child can improve enough to bridge the gap between hopes and marks. An attainable goal is in sight, and it is close enough so striving toward it is apt to be rewarded; in other words, the child can tolerate slight negative feedback and continue working.

To have expectations far above the level justified by one's performance, however, seems to disrupt the feedback system disastrously. Too big a gap between low marks and high expectations is a situation with a bad prognosis. The problem is that feedback is not used; as yet we do not know whether it is distorted, ignored, or seen as irrelevant. The data indicate that, in effect, excessively negative feedback means "no feedback" to first graders.

Interventions

How could expectations be made more realistic, that is, closer to the marks awarded? What steps can be taken? One remedy would be for children to be prepared for school by being made aware in advance that schools give marks across a wide range. Perhaps they could be told what the average mark in reading is likely to be in the school they will attend and what the mark signifies. Or they might even be directly told the mark "most children should expect to get," the strategy being to provide them with some guidelines for their expectations, *not* to force an individual child to hold any particular expectation. Such preparation in kindergarten could play the role of the "reassurance" offered by middle-class parents (see Hess et al., 1968, p. 183) when they tell their four year olds what school will be like.

Rather than preparing children directly, or perhaps in addition to preparing children, parents might be prepared. The parents in the working-class school were inaccurate—like their children, they were too optimistic. Their expectations were more conservative than were expectations of middle-class parents, but they were still overestimates. As a result parents' academic hopes were tarnished in the first formal introduction to school. Overoptimism leaves the parent impotent for generating positive reinforcement, for how can a parent appear happily surprised and praise his child sincerely for getting a C when the parent expected a B? Children are sensitive to parents' genuine feelings. They know intuitively when the parent is sincere and when he is not.

When expectations are too high there are two basic alternatives: raise performance toward expectations or lower expectations toward performance. Boosting performance would be the pleasant solution—everyone would like to see children doing better and performing at or above grade level. The goal of drastically up-grading performance of working-class children has so far proved elusive, however, despite enormous dedication of effort and financial resources. Many very expensive wands have been waved; none yet has been magic.

A second way to boost marks to provide a rapprochement between marks and expectations would be to alter marking standards—either to mark more leniently or to mark with respect to the child's own ability level. Marking on an individual basis also leads to raising the average mark (and so to marking more leniently). In this system a child who tries hard gets a high mark. As we saw, this policy is put in practice by the middle-class school *in first grade*. In second grade, whether or not middle-class school personnel realized it, the standards depended more on actual performance. The gradual abandonment of a marking scale based entirely on effort may be advantageous in that it forecloses abrupt reimposition of the eventually necessary performance-based evaluations.

Another kind of marking strategy might be to ask children what they expect to get and then award marks at least partly on the basis of their expectations. If a child expects a C or D, a B or C may be intensely rewarding and still leave room for improvement later. Problems with this type of marking policy are myriad, of course, including parental fear of favoritism. This strategy is much less appealing than many others.

Still another approach might be to attempt to find a way to report marks that does not distort marking standards and still reduces the psychologically debilitating aspect of large negative discrepances. One such reporting scheme would be to ask teachers to report the range of the quality of performance each child displayed. Teachers could be asked to shade in the appropriate portion of a "mark line" (see figure 7.2). This figure illustrates a report card for a child who is doing very well in reading, very poorly in arithmetic, and about average in conduct. The advantages of this procedure are evident for arithmetic, for there has been no compromise

Figure 7.2
Schematic Report Card for a Child's Range of Academic Performance

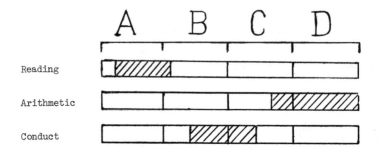

in portraying the child's very low performance, while the child's experienced psychological discrepance may have been reduced to a manageable
level. If the child had expected a B, for instance, the child's experienced
psychological discrepance would likely be the difference between a B and
the *nearest* portion of the shading, namely the shading in the C range rather
than in the D range. By being free to emphasize for himself whatever
portion of the shaded region he chooses, the child could perhaps minimize
his experienced discrepance and so be placed in a position where expectations could improve performance while still being unambiguously in-
formed of his poor arithmetic performance. Once children became accus-
tomed to such a reporting procedure they would also likely develop some
elasticity in the expectation end of the discrepance. Children would come
to expect "about a B" where a little shading into either an A or a C would
be acknowledged as unpredictable. A proposal of this sort looks promising
but, naturally, would require careful scrutiny.

The antithetical policy to anything mentioned so far, that of deliberately lowering children's expectations, is repugnant at first thought. Why
should young children have anything but the highest hopes for themselves?
Anything else belies the American dream. The answer is that lower expectations, i.e., more realistic expectations, may permit a child to process
feedback more adequately and hence to develop greater competence in the
long run.

It may be worth considering lowering children's expectations indirectly by other means. (Attempting to lower children's expectations indirectly by lowering their parent's expectations is not a viable alternative since parents' and children's expectations are not correlated.) The whole process might more appropriately be termed "realistic preparation for school," since the objective would not be to lower expectations indiscriminately but to concentrate on producing *realistic* expectations (which, for a small minority, would even mean increasing expectations) in both parents and children.

At some point the system inexorably will force children's expectations to be realistic. We gather this from the Cohen and Roper data and the Brookover data for older children. It might be good, therefore, to apply a firm but gentle hand early in school to guide expectations in a way that will maximize psychological well-being and simultaneously bring about improved performance, rather than let the scene play itself out to a tragic end of both low performance and low expectations.

ACHIEVEMENT LEVELS

There is considerable confusion in the public mind about subverting "academic excellence" and the use of ranked grading systems. Children, the reasoning goes, should not be given high marks unless they are really performing well. Otherwise the standards of the school will be corrupted to the eventual confusion of all. But the seventh grader who performs well is likely to be the child who has performed well in sixth grade, in fifth grade, and, indeed, all the way back to kindergarten. What led the child to "perform well" in the first place is not so clear. It is not even clear whether the same set of motivations are effective at every age.

Surely the curriculum of the early elementary school is within the mental grasp of all normal children. There is no reason to think most children cannot learn the multiplication tables or learn how to read under proper conditions. "Proper" conditions may mean having expectations for a reasonable degree of success and, for a time, being given positive evaluations in relation to one's own progress rather than in terms of arbitrary standards. In colleges and universities, adherence to marking practices based on objective standards of quality makes sense, say, for classifying future applicants to professional or graduate school. But then the learner may change courses, change schools, or drop out. It does not necessarily make sense to enforce arbitrary standards if the aim is to get a six year old to start reading and to derive enough pleasure from reading to continue to do so.

It may help to make explicit what we meant by the statement that the curriculum of the elementary schools is within the grasp of all normal children. The statement implies an ideal distribution of scholastic achievement of children just graduating from elementary school (figure 7.3), in which only a few children fail to attain grade-level norms in the core areas of reading and arithmetic. The large majority of children should slightly exceed such norms. A modest number of children would even display more advanced performance. How could such a distribution be attained? Literally billions of dollars have been spent trying to bring this about, and we certainly have no ready answer. As we have seen, natural, unguided expectations did not tend to produce this ideal distribution but, rather, tended to boost the performance of the superior middle-class children and (apparently) not help the poorer performing working-class children. Two strands of evidence emphasize the potential importance of teachers' expectations as a way of attaining this ideal distribution.

First, teachers' expectations may not always be "open to evidence" once they have been established. Some teachers (see Palardy, 1969) expect boys to do as well as girls in reading, and boys in their classes do tend to do as well as girls (which is contrary to the usual observation that girls outperform boys in reading). How young children actually perform, in other words, depends on the expectations of teachers, even if those expectations differ from "cultural norms." The beneficial effects of teacher expecta-

Figure 7.3
Ideal Distribution of Scholastic Achievement

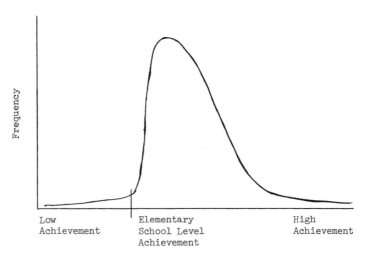

| Low Achievement | Elementary School Level Achievement | High Achievement |

Child's Scholastic Achievement Level

tions can apparently be applied selectively to the less competent children (the poorer-reading sex in the above case), and so provide a way of obtaining the ideal distribution depicted above. Teachers' expectations need not bear any strong relation to the children's present performance, in other words.

Second, even though the Pygmalion studies point to IQ as a prevalent source of teacher expectations, teachers' expectations need not be based on "relevant" criteria. In fact, teachers can and often do form their expectations by considering rather diverse criteria, especially for young children. As the reader has seen, for the first-grade middle-class children in this study there was virtually no relation between IQ and early reading performance, yet middle-class children, by the end of third grade, had achieved the ideal distribution.

To achieve the ideal distribution one must selectively assist poor scholastic performers, not discourage performers who are relatively poor at the start. Teachers' reliance on IQ cues in the earliest days of school would accomplish exactly the opposite, for children with high IQs would receive an extra boost due to high teacher expectations—and they need the boost the least. Early reliance on some other characteristic of the child, say, effort, may be more desirable. There may be some freedom in the choice of the particular dimension to use since, in the Palardy work cited above, teacher expectations were based on a supposed equality of the sexes, and Rist's (1970) and Lambert's (1970) work indicates that teacher expectations may be based on the student's dialect as well as on other social class characteristics.

The Role of Parents

The failure of even elaborate preschool interventions to produce lasting cognitive gains for disadvantaged children has been disappointing. Bronfenbrenner's (1974) careful review of preschool intervention studies (limited to studies in which interventions were evaluated against some kind of control group) points strongly toward parental influence as a crucial variable in program success. (See also Gordon, 1970; Gray and Klaus, 1970; Karnes et al., 1970; Schaeffer, 1969; Bercovia and Feshbach, 1974). The only elementary-school-age study of intervention cited by Bronfenbrenner or known to us (Smith, 1968) agrees that parent involvement in intervention is the crucial element. (A study by Zirkel [1972] involving the enhancement of children's self-concepts also found parental involvement essential.) Even for high schoolers, parental involvement leads to gains for both Mexican-American and Anglo pupils (Anderson and Evans, n.d.).

Hildahl (1972) calls attention to the interaction of class and ability, which we have seen clearly in our microdata. Class and ability could interact all through the life cycle. What has not been very clear until now is that parental influences can interact with IQ and so provide the explanation for how class and ability interact early in a child's school career. Some parents seem to base their expectations on the same attribute of the child (IQ) that will be instrumental in performance. They may therefore reinforce outside school the same behaviors reinforced inside.

But exactly what parents do or what effects parents have on children is not well understood at present. A famous book about child rearing (Yarrow, Campbell, and Burton, 1968, p. 152) concludes with a sobering statement: "The compelling legend of maternal influences on child behavior . . . does not have its roots in solid data and its decisive verification remains . . . a subject for future research." As yet, no one can disagree with this assertion made a decade ago. Whatever parents do to catalyze child behavior is far from clear. Research in this book does brush a few tentative strokes on the empty canvas Yarrow and her colleagues hold up, however. Parents' *expectations* can have some influence.

We saw that middle-class children whose marks changed were apt to be those whose parents' predictions disagreed with their child's initial mark. Children whose parents thought they could do better *did* do better, and vice versa. From what we can tell so far, parents' expectations exert more impact upon middle-class than upon working-class children and more impact in first grade than in second grade in the middle-class school.

There is some suspicion that white parents and black parents form their expectations in different ways, perhaps in ways that make their children react to school differently. Notably, white parents of both social-class levels may use a subjective estimate of IQ, perhaps unconsciously, to gauge their expectations, while black parents do not. It is astounding that high correlations exist between IQ and white parents' expectations and essentially no correlation exists between IQ and black parents' expectations in the present data.

The negligible correspondence between parents' and children's expectations in both first and second grade is puzzling—one would have guessed that parents' expectations governed performance by shaping their children's expectations, but this is not the case. Eventually parents' and children's expectations will tend to converge, even if parental expectations do not directly influence their children's expectations, because both sets of expectations move toward agreement with the children's marks.

Parents, however, remain involved in many potential explanations for the differences in performance between the two school populations. Parents, after all, are the chief mediators of SES-linked effects. Differences between parents noted earlier included the closeness of ties to school, the awareness of school norms for marking, and the like. The strong social-class differences in how parents prepare children for school are well documented by others. Middle-class mothers are aware of and sensitive to the child's need for reassurance when the child begins school (Hess and Shipman, 1965; Hess, Shipman, Brophy, and Bear, 1968). Working-class parents, on the other hand, tend to warn their children about obedience to a new authority figure (the teacher). Proto-academic activities like reading, playing library, or playing school are more frequent in middle-class homes (Bing, 1963), so school may play a marginal role in the socialization of middle-class children compared to the role it plays for working-class children.

There is some evidence, however, that the socialization process that leads to success in school may be the same irrespective of social background level. Greenberg, Shore, and Davidson (1972) found that good achievers had similar readiness, both in the cognitive and affective areas, and that this similarity in "caution and creativity" (p. 381) appeared despite extreme differences in economic level, school, and racial membership. While the "successful formula" may be similar in different social groups it may be much more frequently utilized by some groups than others.

ABSENCE AND PARENT INFLUENCE

Absence rates were correlated with both parents' expectations and children's marks in the working-class school. Middle-class children are absent much less often and, in general, their absences are not related either to performance level or to parents' expectation level. The middle-class parent apparently takes more pains to get a child to school, even if he believes the child is a relatively poor student. Thus absences can be seen as a mediator of effects of parents' expectations in the working-class school but not in the middle-class school. In addition, in the middle-class school parents may keep absences from affecting performance by seeing to it that the child makes up missed work. In both schools we found absences to be almost completely independent of the child's own expectations.

While we are on the subject of absences we should note that in reanalyzing the Coleman (1966) report, Wiley (1973) suggested that differential time spent in school was an important cause of school differences, a cause the report glossed over. Time spent in school could be an important source of inter-school variations; in our data the school with more absenteeism also showed the poorer performance. Some caution should be exercised in producing policy recommendations based on absence data, however, because other researchers disagree with Wiley's conclusion and also point to the likely complexity of the absence variable (see Karweit, 1976, and Douglas and Ross, 1965).

More schooling, measured in hours or days, will not necessarily decrease inter-pupil differences. Increasing days per year or hours per day is not likely, in our view, to abolish educational deficits. In fact, adding to the number of days schools are open would probably increase the disparity between low achievers and high achievers because the absentee rate would be applied to a larger number of school days, leading middle-class children to gain even more (in the same manner that "Sesame Street" increases differences between social classes). Children who are now excessively absent, we suspect, will continue their excessive absenteeism whether school meets nine months or eleven months. It seems more appropriate to get those who are now absent back into the school.

Note also that a number of kinds of "absence" exist in addition to the kind denoted by absence or lateness on report cards. Children in the working-class school may be "absent" from instruction though they are physically present. The teacher, for example, must spend time searching for dry shoes when a child is sent to school without rubbers on a rainy day. Or, for another example, the child with an inadequate breakfast may be apathetic because of hunger; the child is psychologically absent because of a short attention span. These kinds of "absence" plus many others that could be listed mean less time devoted to instruction.

The correlations between absenteeism and marks in the working-class school may indicate that children are responding to different quantities of instruction, but the picture is fuzzy. One obvious loose end is that in the working-class school lateness correlated about as well with children's marks as did absences. Despite the conceptual similarity between absences and lateness, they imply drastically different absence times and, so, from this point of view, should have displayed different correlations with the children's marks.

Epilogue

Sociologists study large collectivities (e.g., occupational groups, labor unions, political parties, ethnic enclaves, even adults bound together to form states and nations) and also smaller groups (e.g., juries, gangs, and school boards). Sociologists have not taken much notice of children in either large- or small-group studies, however. Even in family research, where one might think children and adults would receive equal attention, adults have held the center of the stage. How do *parents* raise children, how do teenagers respond to *parental* pressures—this is the way the questions are phrased. The best-known recent book on how social class affects child rearing, Kohn's *Class and Conformity,* analyzes only data procured from adults. Well and good, but more is needed.

In our society age stratification is becoming more and more rigid. Some hospitals segregate the newborn; some municipalities provide day care for school-age children before and after school; nursing homes for the elderly are everywhere. One consequence of this age segregation is that social innovations focusing directly on children are springing up on all sides: Headstart, Upward Bound, all kinds of day-care programs, not to mention the stratification in programming and content of the mass media. Sociological forces and institutions influence persons from the time of birth onward, not only when persons reach adulthood. The time seems ripe, indeed, overdue, for sociologists to become involved in serious study of sociological development of children in a complex society. The social world of children is a complex structure worthy of theoretical and practical investigation in its own right. This book is one effort in that direction.

An underlying theme of this research has been how the school as a social institution affects expectations of young children. We have provided some answers but many questions remain. Notably, children's interaction with teachers warrants considerably more investigation. A teacher is an enormously important person to her young pupils. It is easy to forget how much time a kindergarten or first-grade child spends with one teacher over a school year. For the child this is compulsory time, and if the child dislikes a teacher he cannot alter the arrangement. The child who complains may even suffer for it.

Modern society thrusts children outside the family early. When children join day-care, nursery, or kindergarten groups, they enter groups that resemble adult work-groups. Most children commute twice a day, eat at least one meal with their fellows, obtain various medical and health services under group auspices, and find considerable entertainment and recreation as well as ''work'' with their group. It may be time for sociologists to take serious account of the extrafamilial experiences of young children. Such contact is now an increasing part of our complex society. Our data suggest classical sociological variables, like the shaping of social-class differences, may be explicated by studying young children.

Nothing much is known about a child's early experiences in group life and group activities—his sociological upbringing, if you will. How does this upbringing affect his later functioning as an adult group member or the nature of adult social groups? Theorists like Mead and Cooley, who talked of the ''looking-glass self,'' supposed that the developing individual shaped a self-image from the reactions of others. A young child's social matrix outside the family provides the first impartial looking-glass. A detailed account of how social process shapes the child and how a child in turn shapes social process, however, remains to be given. In this sense this book has implicitly dealt with child socialization, especially how sociological and demographic factors affect the development of young children.

Also worth noting is the parallel between this research with young children and the many sociological studies that follow high-school students into early adulthood (see, for example, Alexander and Eckland, 1975). A favorite topic of sociologists in the past few years, in fact, has been status attainment. Interest has centered on the variance accounted for by different social precursors such as parent's occupation or education, which are measured when students are in high school. Similar forecasts based on sociological variables might be possible much earlier in the life cycle, although such a strategy is one that has not been tried thus far. The prediction of educational or status attainment using peer plans, parents' desire, school achievement, and the like might be almost as successful forecasting from third grade to adulthood as from high school to adulthood, for the causal role played by the standard predictor variables may be more clearly specified earlier in the life cycle. Peers in high school may be very much like peers in grade school, both in terms of social class and in terms of aspiration levels. The present research suggests that studies of status attainment back up a decade or more.

One thing this book does show is that life trajectories for children are being shaped in the first grade among a complex web of social interrelations we have only begun to untangle. The book gives a few vague hints to explain why resources—personnel and money—in themselves are unlikely to produce changes in children. The book gives a little information on how racial differences in school affect performance, but the ways in which the races were found to be *similar* deserve equal attention. Though such findings do not make headlines, they may prove to be the real news. Passing fads in scholarship may emphasize that the strongest black/white difference to occur in this study was that between the sources of parents' expectations; history may recall that parents' expectations were equal by race despite the fact that the basis for expectations differed.

Three things impress us more and more: one, the early importance of parents in the academic socialization process; two, the variety of implications marking policies have for children's expectations and school performance; and three, the complexity of the world when viewed from the child's eyes.

References

Alexander, K., and B. K. Eckland. 1975. "Contextual effects in the high school attainment process." *American Sociological Review* 40:402–16.

Anderson, J. G., and S. Evans. n.d. "Subcultural differences in child socialization." Mimeograph paper, Department of Psychology, Purdue University.

Bercovici, A., and N. Feshbach. 1974. "Teaching styles of mothers of 'successful' readers and 'problem' readers in the first grade." Paper presented at the annual meetings of the American Educational Research Association, Philadelphia, Pa.

Berger, J., T. L. Conner, and M. H. Fisek, eds. 1974. *Expectation States Theory: A Theoretical Research Program.* Cambridge, Mass.: Winthrop Publishers.

Berger, J., M. Zelditch, Jr., and B. Anderson, eds. 1966. *Sociological Theories in Progress,* vol. 1. Boston: Houghton Mifflin.

Bing, E. 1963. "Effect of childrearing practices on development of differential cognitive abilities." *Child Development* 34:631–48.

Bishop, Y. M. M., S. E. Fienberg, and P. W. Holland. 1975. *Discrete Multivariate Analysis: Theory and Practice.* Cambridge, Mass.: M.I.T. Press.

Bronfenbrenner, U. 1974. "A report on longitudinal evaluations of preschool programs, vol. 2: Is early intervention effective?" DHEW Publication No. (OHD) 74–25. New York: Cornell University.

Brookover, W. B., E. L. Erickson, and L. M. Joiner. 1967. "Self-concept of ability and school achievement, III." U.S. Office of Education, Cooperative Research Project No. 2831. East Lansing: Office of Research and Publications, Michigan State University.

Brookover, W. B., J. LePere, D. Hamachek, S. Thomas, and E. Erickson. 1965. "Self-concept of ability and school achievement, II." U.S. Office of Education, Cooperative Research Project No. 1636. East Lansing: Office of Research and Publications, Michigan State University.

Brookover, W. B., A. Patterson, and J. Shailer. 1962. "Self-concept of ability and school achievement." U.S. Office of Education, Cooperative Research Project No. 845. East Lansing: Office of Research and Publications, Michigan State University.

Brookover, W. B., S. Thomas, and A. Patterson. 1964. "Self-concept of ability and school achievement." *Sociology of Education* 37:271–78.

Cohen, E. G. 1972. "Interracial interaction disability." *Human Relations* 25:9–24.

Cohen, E. G., and S. Roper. 1972. "Modification of interracial interaction disability." *American Sociological Review* 37:643–57.

Coleman, J. S. 1961. *The Adolescent Society.* New York: Free Press.

Coleman, J. S., E. Q. Campbell, C. J. Hobson, J. McPartland, A. M. Mood, F. D. Weinfeld, and R. L. York. 1966. *Equality of Educational Opportunity.* Washington, D.C.: U.S. Government Printing Office.

Crandall, V. 1969. "Sex differences in expectancy of intellectual and academic reinforcement." In *Achievement Related Motives in Children,* ed. C. P. Smith, pp. 11–45. New York: Russell Sage.

Dickstein, E. 1972. "The development of self-esteem: theory and measurement." Unpublished doctoral dissertation, Department of Psychology, The Johns Hopkins University.

Dornbusch, S. M., and W. R. Scott. 1975. *Evaluation and the Exercise of Authority.* San Francisco: Jossey-Bass.

Douglas, J. W. B., and J. M. Ross. 1965. "The effects of absence on primary school performance." *The British Journal of Educational Psychology* 35:28–40.

Entwisle, D. R. 1975. "Sociological understanding versus policy design and intervention: The adolescent crisis." In *Social Policy and Sociology,* ed. N. J. Demerath, O. Larsen, and K. Schuessler, pp. 243–49. New York: Academic Press.

Entwisle, D. R., and L. A. Hayduk. 1977. "Academic Expectations and the School Attainment of Young Children." Paper presented at the annual meetings of the American Psychological Association, San Francisco.

Entwisle, D. R., and M. Webster. 1974a. "Raising children's expectations for their own performance: A classroom application." In *Expectation States Theory: A Theoretical Research Program,* ed. J. Berger, T. L. Conner, and M. H. Fisek, Chapter 7. Cambridge, Mass.: Winthrop Publishers.

———. 1974b. "Expectations in mixed racial groups." *Sociology of Education* 47:301–18.

Feld, S. 1975. Personal communication.

Feldman, R. S., and V. L. Allen. 1974. "Four studies on attribution of ability." Technical Report No. 281. Madison: Wisconsin R. & D. Center for Cognitive Learning, The University of Wisconsin.

Gordon, I. J. 1970. *Parent Participation in Compensatory Education.* Urbana: University of Illinois Press.

Gray, S., and R. Klaus. 1970. *Early Training Project: The Seventh Year Report.* Nashville, Tenn.: John F. Kennedy Center for Research on Education and Human Development, George Peabody College for Teachers.

Greenberg, J. W., M. S. Shore, and H. H. Davidson. 1972. "Caution and creativity as correlates of achievement in disparate social-racial groups." *Journal of Negro Education* 41:377–82.

Hess, R. D., and V. Shipman. 1965. "Early experience and socialization of cognitive modes in children." *Child Development* 36:869–86.

Hess, R. D., V. Shipman, J. E. Brophy, and R. M. Bear. 1968. "The cognitive environments of preschool children." Unpublished manuscript, Graduate School of Education, University of Chicago.

Hildahl, S. H. 1972. "The allocation function of education in the United States." *International Journal of Comparative Sociology* 13:141–49.

Husèn, T. 1969. *Talent, Opportunity and Career*. Stockholm: Almqvist and Wiksell.

Jensen, A. R. 1973. *Educability and Group Differences*. New York: Harper and Row.

Karnes, M., J. Teska, A. Hodgins, and E. Badger. 1970. "Educational intervention at home by mothers of disadvantaged infants." *Child Development* 41:925–35.

Karweit, N. L. 1976. "A reanalysis of the effect of quantity of schooling on achievement." *Sociology of Education* 49:236–46.

Kohn, M. 1969. *Class and Conformity*. Homewood, Ill.: The Dorsey Press.

Kraus, P. E. 1973. *Yesterday's Children*. New York: Wiley.

Lambert, N. 1970. "Paired associate learning, social status, and tests of logical concrete behavior as univariate and multivariate predictors of first-grade reading achievement." *American Educational Research Journal* 7:511–28.

Lamy, M. W. 1965. "Relation of self-perceptions of early primary children to achievement in reading." In *Human Development Readings in Research,* ed. J. J. Gordon, p. 251. Chicago: Scott, Foresman.

Lesser, G. S. 1972. "Learning, teaching, and television production for children: The experience of Sesame Street." *Harvard Educational Review* 42:232–72.

Maryland State Department of Education. 1975. Maryland Accountability Program Report, School Year 1973–1974. Maryland State Department of Education.

Morse, R. 1967. "Self-concept of ability and school achievement: A comparative study of Negro and Caucasian students." In "Self-Concept of Ability and School Achievement, III," W. B. Brookover, E. L. Erickson, and L. M. Joiner. U.S. Office of Education, Cooperative Research Project No. 2831. East Lansing: Office of Research and Publications, Michigan State University.

Mosteller, F., and R. R. Bush. 1954. "Selected quantitative techniques." In *Handbook of Social Psychology,* ed. G. Lindzey. Cambridge, Mass.: Addison-Wesley.

Mussen, P., J. Conger, and J. Kagan. 1963. *Child Development and Personality* 2d ed. New York: Harper and Row.

Palardy, J. M. 1969. "What teachers believe—what children achieve." *Elementary School Journal* 69:370–74.

Rist, R. C. 1970. "Student social class and teacher expectations: The self-fulfilling prophecy in ghetto education." *Harvard Educational Review* 40:411–51.

Rosenberg, M., and R. A. Simmons. 1971. *Black and White Self-Esteem.* Washington, D.C.: American Sociological Association Rose Monograph Series.

Rotter, J. B. 1966. "Generalized expectancies for internal versus external control of reinforcement." *Psychological Monographs* 80 (whole no. 609).

Schaefer, E. S. 1969. "Home tutoring program." *Children* 16:59–61.

Simpson, C. 1975. "The Social Construction of Ability in Elementary School Classrooms." Unpublished dissertation, Department of Sociology, Stanford University, April 1975.

Smith, M. B. 1968. "School and home: Focus on achievement." In *Developing Programs for the Educationally Disadvantaged,* ed. A. H. Passow, pp. 89–107. New York: Teachers College Press.

Wattenberg, W. W., and C. Clifford. 1964. "Relation of self-concepts to beginning achievement in reading." *Child Development* 35:461–67.

Wiley, D. E. 1973. "Another hour, another day: Quantity of schooling; a potent path for policy." Studies of Educative Processes, Report no. 3, University of Chicago.

Williams, Trevor. 1976. "Teacher prophecies and the inheritance of inequality." *Sociology of Education* 49:223–36.

Wilson, A. B. 1963. "Social stratification and academic achievement." In *Education in Depressed Areas,* ed. A. H. Passow. New York: Teachers College Press.

Yarrow, M. R., J. D. Campbell, and R. V. Burton. 1968. *Child Rearing.* San Francisco: Jossey-Bass.

Zirkel, P. A. 1972. "Enhancing the self-concept of disadvantaged students." *California Journal of Educational Research* 23:125–37.

Index

Absence, 16, 79–80, 115–17, 123, 151–52, 183–84; correlations with other measures, 80, 116; by race, 116; by sex, 116
Academic self-concept, 4–5, 7, 10, 174
Achievement: differences in, 165; ideal distribution of, 180; levels of, 179–81; stability of, 164, 173, 186; standardized, 16, 80–84, 117–18, 151, 154–55; standardized, with IQ controlled, 85–87
Affective bias, 140
Age, effects of, 8

Bishop, Fienberg, and Holland, 22, 24
Buoyancy effect, 39, 41, 68, 104, 143; and regression, 69

Ceiling effects, 35, 104, 139–40
Children's expectations, 1–2, 6, 7, 13, 28–29, 32–36, 126–35, 156, 161, 163–76, 182; and absences, 79–80, 116, 152; changes in, 7, 29, 48, 60, 62–67, 95, 133–35, 144, 153, 173; and control, 170–72; development of, 4–7, 143–44, 173; differences of, by social class, 128–30; differentiation of, by area, 130–31, 148; and evaluation, 1, 3; and lateness, 116, 152; level of, 165–68; and marks, in working-class school, 99–102; measure of, 13–14, 22; and peer ratings, 53, 87, 112, 151; and race, 93–95, 110–11, 132–33, 174–76; raising of, 1; reliability of, 126, 128, 130; and self-esteem, 53, 76–77; and sex, 49, 149–50; timing of observation of, 8–9; validity of, 35, 40, 126–32, 139, 160; in working-class school, 98, 102, 128–30
Children's expectations in middle-class school, 128–30; basis for, 36, 143–44; correlation of, with IQ, 30; in different areas, 65; effect of marks on, 36; lability of, 39; matching, over time, 63; persistence in, 32; in second grade, 59–61, 134–35; and standardized achievement, 82
Classroom effects, 7

Cohort: combined, xiii, 28–29, 52, 81; differences in IQ-mark correlations within, 30; differences within, 10, 103; effects of, 8; and *Maryland Accountability Program Report,* 22–24; middle-class, 27; second-grade, 59; working-class, 93
Coleman report, 4, 172, 183
Collinearity, 69
Consistency: between expectations, 62; over grades, 69; increase in, 46; between marks and expectations, 32–34, 37–39, 48, 58, 92, 103; in teachers' marks, 65, 101, 138
Control, 173, 175; function, 171; internal and external, 163, 170–71; personal, 170–72; and social class, 172–74
Crystallization, 163, 168–70

Design of research, 7
Development of expectations, 1, 2, 4, 5, 7, 10
Dickstein, E., 16, 53
Discrepance, 25, 29, 36–38, 42, 47, 60, 65–70, 71–72, 95, 103–5, 119, 137, 141–46, 148, 153, 157, 160, 172, 176–77; as a causal variable, 46; extreme, 103; as a predictor, 57; reduction, 40
Distar, 104, 136, 145, 159

Ecological validity, 2
Efficacy, 170, 173
Evaluation, 1, 3, 5, 51, 104, 126, 135–36, 139, 158, 166, 170, 175, 179
Experiments: field, xiii, 1, 133, 160; "natural," 144

Feedback, 7, 10, 48, 72, 135–36, 138–39, 141, 144–45, 155, 157, 159, 162, 164–65, 167, 176; effects of, 36–42, 103–6, 143–46; erroneous, 39; model, 5–6, 8; repeated, 72
Floor effects, 35, 139

Grade-level equivalents, 117

Halo effect, 139–40
High expectations, 2, 4, 35, 36, 74, 92, 101, 103, 126, 129–30, 142, 145–46, 153, 166–67, 172–75

191

Library of Congress Cataloging in Publication Data

Entwisle, Doris R
     Too great expectations.

     Includes bibliographical references.
     1. Education, Primary—United States. 2. Students'
socio-economic status—United States. 3. Students—
United States—Attitudes. 4. Child development.
I. Hayduk, Leslie Alec, joint author. II. Title.
LA219.E57   372.9 '73   77-23344
ISBN 0-8018-1986-5